Recreational L
Managemer

Recreational Land Management

Second edition

W. Seabrooke

Professor of Land Economy
Department of Land and Construction Management
University of Portsmouth

and

C. W. N. Miles

Emeritus Professor of Land Management
University of Reading

E & FN SPON
An Imprint of Chapman & Hall

London · Glasgow · New York · Tokyo · Melbourne · Madras

Published by E & FN Spon, an imprint of Chapman & Hall, 2–6 Boundary Row, London SE1 8HN

Chapman & Hall, 2–6 Boundary Row, London SE1 8HN, UK

Blackie Academic & Professional, Wester Cleddens Road, Bishopbriggs, Glasgow G64 2NZ, UK

Chapman & Hall Inc., 29 West 35th Street, New York NY10001, USA

Chapman & Hall Japan, Thomson Publishing Japan, Hirakawacho Nemoto Building, 6F, 1-7-11 Hirakawa-cho, Chiyoda-ku, Toyko 102, Japan

Chapman & Hall Australia, Thomas Nelson Australia, 102 Dodds Street, South Melbourne, Victoria 3205, Australia

Chapman & Hall India, R.Seshadri, 32 Second Main Road, CIT East, Madras 600 035, India

First edition 1977
Second edition 1993

© 1993 W. Seabrooke and C.W.N. Miles

Typeset in 10/12 Times by Blackpool Typesetting Services Ltd, Blackpool
Printed in Great Britain by Page Brothers, Norwich

ISBN 0 419 13500 6   0 442 31687 9 (USA)

A catalogue record for this book is available from the British Library

Library of Congress Cataloging-in-Publication data available

Contents

Preface

The science or art of management is applied to virtually every human activity, whether it be as prosaic as arranging a family day out or as complex as the establishment and running of a successful business. In the former case management is probably best described as 'organization', but in the latter it involves much more than organization, consisting of research, planning, understanding of the medium, anticipation, analysis and perseverance at the very least.

Some of these aspects of management are common to every endeavour and can be followed by simple rule of thumb; others are more sophisticated, requiring more objective, deliberate and perhaps specific application. Some are almost unique in the way they are applied with skilled professional judgement to each undertaking. Most of the principles of management can be taught but because, to a greater or lesser degree, each type of enterprise is different and because each individual enterprise within the same type is in some respects unique, the practice of management must use theory as just one ingredient to be applied with intelligence to the real world which lies at the manager's fingertips. Theory should provide a robust framework enabling the manager to:

- undertake the basic and predictable steps toward the successful management of an enterprise;
- analyse when, where, why and how things have gone awry.

This book does not suggest fixed lines along which the management of any particular business must run, but it does try to set out the specialities involved in setting up and running a countryside recreational venture, from its first conception to its establishment and successful operation. Readers will not learn from this book the fixed rules of recreational land management, for there are no secret formulae. They should, however, gain an appreciation of some of the principles upon which a management plan may be based and be made aware of the philosophical background of that opportunity which, if successfully exploited, will enhance their own and many other people's quality of life.

An introduction to recreational land use

1

1.1 DEFINITION AND EVOLUTION

The purpose of this book is to discuss the development and management of land for recreation. It is only coincidentally concerned with the extent to which a recreational use may be more appropriate or less appropriate than a non-recreational use. The term 'recreational land use' is a generic description denoting specific activities and pursuits, which may range from informal recreation in the countryside to more formalized leisure pursuits in an urban setting such as a sports complex, cinema or gambling casino. Recreation does not fit comfortably with some of the conventional criteria used to stereotype land uses. Distinctions between rural and urban land uses may be blurred – recreational enterprises embrace developments of an urban nature in a rural setting and green open-space within an urban setting. There is wide variation in the life cycle of recreation enterprises: obsolescence may quickly render some worthless while others may endure for generations. The full spectrum of activities which may fall within the category of recreation is very broad. Consequently, a correspondingly wide variety of opportunities, expectations, constraints and pitfalls must be appreciated by the manager of land to be used for recreation.

Recreation is sometimes claimed to be an essential component of life; the philosopher John Locke claimed it to be a civil right. If that is so, it comes well down the ranking of the necessities of life, after the physiological requirements of human existence have been met. This hierarchy of needs was recognized by Adam Smith and, more recently, by Maslow (1943), who postulated that human needs follow an orderly pattern in which the foremost is nourishment followed by shelter and security. Until the basic needs are met there is little concern for recreation. Once they are met, however, the need for love, self esteem and self fulfilment emerge and leisure and recreation become important components of life.

The long-term commitment of land and buildings to accommodate leisure and recreational facilities is largely a phenomenon of post-industrial society. In a newly industrialized Victorian Britain, long working hours left little time for relaxation. Outings on rest-days were hampered by lack of transport, consequently entertainment was sought largely within the confines of the urban areas. Music-halls and, subsequently, picture-houses flourished and other forms of group entertainment – spectator sports in particular – rapidly gained popularity. The separation of participation from entertainment became quite marked as recreational provision responded to popular demand. Nevertheless, social provision became motivated by public welfare considerations. The Factories Act paved the way towards improving the lot of the work force. Paid leisure time in the form of annual holidays meant that holidays away from home no longer remained the prerogative of the wealthy. Even so, the tradition of 'wakes' or 'feast' weeks in many industrial areas encouraged and maintained the emphasis on group recreation. As the road and rail networks expanded and new forms of personal transport such as the bicycle became more widely available, recreational opportunities outside the towns became more accessible. Although participation in recreational activities is far from new, the social changes of the twentieth century have had marked effects on participation in leisure and recreation.

The terms 'leisure' and 'recreation' are often considered synonymous. The former, however, is a more embracing term which includes self-imposed inactivity whereas the latter presupposes some activity designed to enhance self-expression and self-esteem. The greatest proportion of discretionary time available for leisure and recreational pursuits now appears to be spent inside the home rather than outside. In the case of home-based recreation, the need for special facilities in the form of land and buildings is negligible although the need for other hardware may be considerable. Nevertheless, it remains almost axiomatic that other popular forms of recreation do *not* occur in the home; a pint of beer or glass of wine consumed at home is less overtly recreational than the same thing consumed in the surroundings of a pub or wine bar, as part of a social gathering. The social and physical setting is of central importance to participation in leisure and recreation outside the home. This introduces the need for special facilities to accommodate the setting which accompanies the participation.

The nature of urban development in Britain, even now, is such that the change from densely populated, intensively developed areas to more sparsely populated countryside, largely unencumbered by buildings, often occurs over quite short distances. Though most of the population still remains dependent on towns for work and shelter, former dependence has become substantially eroded in the case of leisure and recreation. Most of us can reach different surroundings relatively easily and a choice of recreational opportunities is available to large numbers of people.

Affluence, mobility and free time stimulate demands for greater access to the countryside which some consider to be part of their birthright. However, the countryside in question may be owned or occupied by someone unwilling to grant such access. During the early part of this century increased access to the countryside was actively resisted by many private landowners, who saw this movement as a threat to their own rights and powers: the Battle of Kinder Scout in the Peak District in 1886 was one example of this conflict. Little happened to disturb the status quo (based on private land ownereship) until well into the present century. As part of the welfare movement which pushed for the introduction of improvements in social and working conditions and the imposition of control on urban development, concern was also expressed over preserving and safeguarding the countryside from the erosion caused by urban expansion and making those parts of the countryside not given over to farming, forestry, mineral extraction, water storage, military and other uses, available for public enjoyment.

The Law of Property Act, 1925 granted access to common land for air and exercise but did not address the matter of privately owner land. In 1942 the Scott Report (Ministry of Works and Planning, 1942; see also Cherry, 1975) made extensive comment on the future use of rural land for agriculture and recreation.This gave support to the notion that areas of outstanding countryside should be protected on behalf of the nation under the designation of National Parks. However, little more happened in this respect until 1949; even the Town and Country Planning Act, 1947, which laid the foundation for modern town planning, omitted all but superficial reference to the countryside, squandering an important opportunity to consider the interdependence of town and country. The National Parks and Access to the Countryside Act, 1949 may be considered the first outright statement of interest by the government in the importance of safeguarding, at least part of the countryside of England and Wales. However, it lacked the political power of its 1947 forerunner and gave inadequate attention to how its policies could be effectively implemented or to how its effectiveness could be measured. The lack of autonomy of all but one of the National Park Authorities which were subsequently established is anomalous. Despite the national importance of these parks, after the designation of the first National Park the controlling influence over their administration was ceded to the local authorities, whose role is, ultimately, to act in the best local interest.

The spirit of the 1949 Act was reinforced by the Countryside Act, 1968. This established further guidelines for designating and protecting additional areas of countryside because of their 'outstanding natural beauty' or because they accommodated Sites of Special Scientific Interest. It also provided for the establishment of the Countryside Commission for England and Wales (the Countryside Commission for Scotland was established under a separate Act). Both Commissions were given powers to advise, experiment and counsel in matters of recreation and in protection of the countryside.

However, all this legislation contains an unresolved paradox which leads to a land use dilemma revolving around the distinction between recreation (implying public participation and enjoyment) and preservation or conservation (implying land use control even to the exclusion of recreation) and the extent to which the two are mutually exclusive. Official designations of outstandingly valuable countryside act as a powerful magnet to casual visitors as well as to those actively seeking the qualities which gave rise to the designation, thus subjecting the areas in question to greater pressure than they might otherwise attract. More recent legislation, the Wildlife and Countryside Act, 1981, perpetuates this dilemma.

The demands on the land and natural resources of the industrialized nations appear to have increased more during the twentieth century than over any other equivalent period. In predominantly urban society land is called upon not only to supply food and raw materials but also to accommodate the industrial, commercial and service uses upon which its economic development and the welfare of its citizens is based. Such development involves a conversion of land from its virgin state to a modified state better suited to a more appropriate economic use. The greater the modification, the more remote the original nature of the land becomes and the more difficult (and more expensive) it is to restore the original use. This process of land use development becomes determined not by natural factors but by the impact of physical, social or economic obsolescence. The conversion of countryside to urban uses is a particularly critical threshold in this respect, though even within the context of 'countryside', extensive modification to long established, essentially stable ecosystems can and still does occur with increasing frequency.

Somewhat paradoxically, the country-dweller has become increasingly dependent on the town for the provision of goods, services and entertainment while the town-dweller turns increasingly to the countryside for informal recreation, to experience the historical heritage left by the landed aristocracy of a bygone age and as a natural setting for holidays and pastimes. Recreation in the countryside does create special problems, not least of which is a reticence among some country-folk to welcome, willingly, their urban counterparts. While towns'-people increasingly demand, often with justification, greater access to the countryside some insensitively insist that access be accompanied by urban paraphernalia out of keeping with the rural environment.

If the need for recreation is justifiable, the next question is 'can a suitable site be made available both physically and economically?'; followed by 'to what extent will the ''raw'' site have to be modified to enable it to meet the precise need in the most economic way?'. These questions raise further issues, for example:

- can demand be properly measured?
- can it be accurately expressed in land use terms?
- who owns or controls the site?
- do conflicting legal interests or obligations exist over it?
- what are the probable development costs?
- can these be defrayed by grants or subsidies?
- how much will it cost to operate the site?
- how should the performance of the enterprise be monitored to ensure an appropriate return for the land?

Private landowners have for centuries had a well developed interest in the recreational use of their estates. More recently, as both central and local government became active landowners and as their powers over the control and implementation of land use policies extended, each has taken a more positive interest in the provision of recreation for the general public. Even more recently leisure and tourism have become economically 'respectable' spheres of operation for commercial developers in the sense that it is no longer uncommon to find such development schemes being funded by financial institutions.

Without a full appreciation of the competing and complementary demands for the use of land, a land manager is in a poor position to make a rational decision about appropriate uses and their implementation. Recreation is but one among many possible uses. The varied demands of recreation seekers introduce increased and possibly conflicting demands, competing for space with farming and forestry. The management of these production orientated enterprises is concentrated on increasing efficiency of production. Management has become less intuitive, objectives have become more explicit to the extent that primary objectives are often adhered to with a single-mindedness which precludes subordinate or tangential objectives. Indeed, farmers and foresters have been criticized for overlooking the public's expectation that they have a long term responsibility of stewardship toward the countryside; but attitudes are changing. There is some evidence that public pressure has caused something of an alteration in some farming practices, for example, the restoration of public rights of way after ploughing. More particularly, economic pressure on the farming industry itself has resulted in a need for farmers to examine their costs carefully and in many cases to alter or reduce their inputs. Further economic pressure may result in a reduction in the total area of land used for agricultural production, indeed, public sector funding has been targeted at the withdrawal of land from agricultural use and the stimulation of provision of non-agricultural services in the rural economy. The appearance and use of certain areas of land may alter dramatically over the next decade.

1.2 RECREATIONAL PROVISION FOR PUBLIC USE

The use of land and facilities for recreational purposes by the general public has already been referred to on several occasions. It may be as well, therefore, to distinguish between 'public' and 'private' use. Public use presupposes that the public at large has the opportunity to gain access to and use the facilities in question. Ostensible discrimination exists only in so far as a cost is involved which some can afford and others cannot.

Although in this sense public use exists irrespective of the status (namely public or private) of the landowner, it is often assumed that, for some reason 'public' facilities must be publicly owned as well as being available for the use of the general public. Where the public sector controls the utilization of a site it does so either through the ownership of a legal interest in the land or possibly by some management agreement. Where the private sector controls utilization it does so similarly through the ownership of a legal interest. Public or private sector control may each permit enjoyment of the site by the general public or private individuals. Private use is synonymous with privileged use and presupposes specific individual rights of use exercised primarily by those selected by the controller of the facilities in question. Rights of use can be conveyed in numerous ways including invitation or membership of an accepted organization. The primary concern of this book is the public use of facilities whether on publicly or privately owned land. Although the specific criteria against which management performance is judged may vary between public sector and private sector landowners, to claim that this must of necessity give rise to fundamental differences in the management discipline governing the management of land in the two sectors is manifestly spurious and may, therefore, be viewed as an excuse for management inadequacies.

The public sector has, for many years, been active in providing recreation facilities at national and local levels in urban and rural areas. Much of this provision typifies the principle that provision should respond to need rather than demand. Need tends to be expressed in terms of participation rates for readily identifiable, even stereotyped facilities. The inadequacies of this approach were expressed in 1967 in the *Pilot National Recreation Survey* published by the British Tourist Authority (British Travel Association/ University of Keele, 1967). The report of the survey pointed out that

> there is no 'national' recreational man (or woman) whose use of leisure may be taken as typical for the country as a whole: in fact recreation appears to be one of these characteristics of our national population that varies profoundly on a regional scale. There is no stereotyped national pattern in our use of spare time, only a set of completely varying patterns, strongly idiosyncratic, and themselves probably composed of even more intricate sub-regional and local variations . . .

Aggregation to the scale of the 'Standard Region' involves a first stage of generalization with some loss of sharpness of focus: further aggregation of major regional contrasts to yield a single national pattern blurs the image still further; though clearly for many purposes the generalized national picture is the relevant one, and indeed a necessary frame of reference for more detailed analysis on a finer regional scale. In short, the patterns of recreational activity in Britain are a mosaic and only quite local studies are likely to reveal its full detail.

Further examination of the stereotyped nature of much public-sector provision leads to the suggestion that this is not through inherent lack of imagination (quite the contrary in many instances). The practical manifestation of the judgement of the British Travel Association survey is that recreational provision will be based on the most basic of common denominators and resulting, for example, 'in a simple' natural site and access to it.

In making land available for outdoor recreation the public sector may, initially at least, provide only basic facilities, leaving users of the site to do what they like on it. This level of provision has now come to be regarded as a free good; it has also, incidentally, led to the criticism that these facilities cater for the better-off, being those best equipped to make use of basic facilities. Clearly, when members of the public are required to pay for recreation, they expect to receive more than they could get elsewhere free of charge. Commercial enterprises must, therefore, go beyond the provision of the most basic facilities (unless they are unique in character or occurrence) and develop facilities which rely less on the inventiveness and resourcefulness of the participants. This then becomes less concerned with 'need' than with the economic concept of demand and all the management problems this entails, in particular, the translation of demand into specific enterprises and facilities.

It may be argued that the response of the private sector to the demand for recreation may be similar but the reasons influencing the final result may be quite different. The demand for recreation may be regarded simply as a social phenomenon but if it is also regarded as an economic pheonomenon then it may represent commercial potential. The level of provision typified by permitting access to a site comes at the bottom of the ladder of private provision and is usually justified on one of two grounds. Many landowners hold the view that the general public should be afforded access to the property of which they are custodian to enjoy the amenity of a privileged inheritance; this view arises out of paternalism or to demonstrate a social responsibility. Another reason might be force of circumstance which applies when a landowner has received financial consideration (usually from the State in the form of grants or tax allowances) which is conditional upon reasonable public access to the property being granted.

Providing specific facilities for recreation and leisure entails facing the problem of assessing demand and, subsequently, finding and justifying the application of the capital necessary to enable that demand to be exploited. While the commercially minded landowner faces problems similar to those encountered by the public sector, additional commercial considerations must be faced which the public sector may be able to avoid.

In the private sector a recreational enterprise will be established, by and large, as a business venture but may, nevertheless, be fulfilling a greater function than just achieving a profit. If successful it will be fulfilling a need or desire although it may, in the first place, have set out to stimulate or focus that demand. Making a profit should not necessarily detract from the wider benefits of a landowner making his land available for the enjoyment of the public: it is unlikely that the enterprise would have existed at all if run at a loss. Even where privately owned facilities do appear to be run at a loss there is usually some quasi-commmercial benefit to be had somewhere, for example, a non-priced country park on a private estate may minimize costs of trespass or over-use elsewhere on the estate.

The era of the individual owner of extensive country estates has been drawing to a close since the beginning of this century. Non-farming owners have been substantially replaced by a larger number of owner-occupiers. It is a matter of the wider distribution of ownership interests among a number of people and bodies and of some substitution of individual owners by institutional owners (in various guises) and, to a lesser extent, by public sector owners. Such a dissipation of interests does not cause them to disappear, nor does it wipe out the responsibility of the controllers of those interests to provide opportunities for the proper enjoyment of the countryside by the population at large. It is, and will increasingly be, a matter of who is to exercise that particular responsibility of landownership.

Where legal ownership and occupation rests in smaller units than formerly, the opportunity for the private individual to initiate a sizeable recreational enterprise will diminish. This is not to say that the smaller, more specialized or intensive enterprise will disappear, nor that the private sector is to be dismissed as too small or irrelevant. Indeed, with financial pressures being what they are today a recreational enterprise, imaginatively and carefully run, may well be something which not only fulfils an owner's duty to the public, but also helps to provide funds for the upkeep of less viable portions of the estate and for the repair and improvement of other property in the owner's care.

Although at the date of writing, no tax surcharge is payable on investment income (and as a consequence rental income as such is no more severely taxed than is earned income), the measurement of trading income for taxation purposes is less severe than that of investment income. There is more opportunity for income and capital growth – and more exposure to the risk of failure – by operating a business rather than simply investing in the land or capital supporting it. Thus the active use of land by its proprietor may have its attractions. Furthermore, ancillary recreational use of a farm by the farmer may produce a much greater return than can be wrested from the land by growing crops or keeping livestock (hence the contention that a crop of caravans is more remunerative than a crop of corn). Indeed, both landowner and farmer may find that a particular recreational use can be run alongside or as a regular alternative to another.

1.3 CONSIDERATION OF SITES FOR RECREATIONAL USES

Land, by its very nature, is a non-homogeneous commodity (its location, if nothing else, makes it unique) and although sites may be similar they cannot be perfect substitutes for each other. The owner is not just faced with a demand for 'recreation' or 'amenity' but with a demand associated with a particular site. He or she is concerned not only with the general level of demand for an activity but more specifically with the proportion of potential demand that will direct itself (with or without encouragement) to that site to obtain this intangible commodity: recreation. Even the most innocuous proposals for the use of a site for recreation can arouse bitter opposition, often from local residents who are at once and understandably afraid that their peace will be shattered by an influx of unwanted visitors, while at the same time the proposals will be welcomed by others who see the enterprise generating local employment.

In a perfect world, no doubt, recreational enterprises would be perfectly distributed to reflect demand. However, many leisure enterprises arise simply because a site is available, ideal or not, and an operator attempts to make the best of it. It may be argued that an entrepreneur with a development idea in mind can search and search for the ideal site before developing. However, once the development takes place, time and Murphy's Law (that if something can go wrong it will go wrong) will conspire to make the site less than ideal. Subsequent management of the site will, nevertheless, still have to take account of the relative suitability of the site.

The land manager should be able to identify, systematically and objectively, the potential use of any site, the likely duration of that use, and the capacity of the site to accommodate recreational pressures. However, value is the yardstick by which management effectiveness is measured. The value of the land use is measured by reference to the difference between the value of the benefits arising from the use in question and the value of the costs directly attributable to it.

Management values are normally measured in conventionalized units which facilitate comparison. In recreation, benefits are often measured in simple money terms or in some unit of consumption (sales) per customer. The costs involved in providing a leisure service may seem self evident but many recreation enterprises rely on some element of uniqueness and the more unique the resources, the less readily can they be measured by reference to standardized values (such as market value). In these circumstances the manager may have to resort to alternative values on which to base decisions; for example, opportunity costs may be utilized by estimating the market value of the resources in their next best use. Ultimately, the value placed on a site by its owner will be governed by the owner's own perception of it. Indeed, it should be recognized that many of the attributes of the landscape so prized today are a legacy of previous owners who adopted individualistic, idiosyncratic views of their property which became reflected in its subsequent management.

REFERENCES

British Travel Association/University of Keele (1967) *Pilot National Recreation Survey*, British Tourist Authority, London.

Cherry, G.E. (1975) *Environmental Planning 1939–1969, Vol. II National Parks and Recreation in the Countryside*, HMSO, London.

Maslow, A.H. (1943) A Theory of Human Motivation. *Psychological Review*, **50**, 370–96.

Ministry of Works and Planning (1942) *Report of the Committee on Land Utilisation in Rural Areas*, HMSO, London.

The institutional framework of public sector provision of recreation

2

The public sector plays a dual role in the provision of facilities for leisure and recreation. The provision and management of recreation enterprises for public enjoyment is the more direct but the public sector also provides an organizational framework which influences provision by the private sector. The main spheres of influence are:

- financial support;
- advice;
- development control of one form or another;
- active participation in development and management.

2.1 NATIONAL ORGANIZATIONS

The specific bodies active in the public sector change from time to time and their level of influence changes correspondingly. For example, water authorities, once part of the public sector are now private sector organizations. The list of organizations below is not intended to be definitive but to illustrate the scope of public sector influence at a national level.

> The Countryside Commission
> The English Tourist Board
> The Sports Council
> English Nature
> English Heritage (Cadw in Wales)
> British Waterways Board
> The Forestry Commission
> National Park Authorities

This list does more to demonstrate the fragmented and unco-ordinated nature of national policy toward recreation than to demonstrate comprehensive commitment. Of the bodies included in the list, the Countryside Commission, English Nature, English Heritage and the Sports Council fall within the broad ambit of the Department of the Environment while the Forestry Commission resides firmly within the Ministry of Agriculture, Fisheries, and Food. The Sports Council is in an unusual position in that there is a government minister with specific responsibility for sport. The Countryside Commission, for example, could hardly be classed as a provider of recreational facilities though it gives advice and grant aid in certain circumstances. The English Tourist Board appears most in evidence through its regional and local organization. The Sports Council is almost in the same category although it does own and manage some facilities, essentially training facilities regarded as centres of excellence in particular areas of sport. Purists may challenge the inclusion of National Parks in a list of national organizations; in many respects the term is a misnomer. For example, it does not describe an organization but an area of land over which a particular type of 'local authority' has limited jurisdiction; it is a national designation but essentially a local phenomenon as is, for example, an 'Area of Outstanding Natural Beauty'.

The Forestry Commission is responsible for one of the largest landholdings in the country although, under Government instruction it has sold off some of its smaller land holdings. Established in 1919 to promote and ensure the establishment of woodland for commercial timber production, its aims have been extended by subsequent legislation relating to forestry and the countryside. Much greater emphasis is now put on the requirement that, where possible and suitable, Forestry Commission property should be made available for public leisure and recreation. There are examples where the Commission has gone even further and developed specific facilities for leisure and tourism.

English Nature may appear rather out of place in this list because it has little or no direct interest in recreation, its main concern being the conservation of the natural environment. Nevertheless, the conservation movement has many active supporters (this applies to several aspects of our heritage, not just the natural) and English Nature, in providing nature reserves and safeguarding Sites of Special Scientific Interest provides a valuable recreational asset for those members of the public who derive recreation from their active support of the conservation movement.

2.1.1 The Countryside Commission

The Wildlife and Countryside Act, 1981 changed the status of the Countryside Commission but not, fundamentally, its functions. It is a body corporate having the status of a 'grant in aid' body. It employs its own staff and it receives a block grant which it is free to spend as it determines within the range of its functions. However, this freedom is constrained to the extent that the Commission is dependent on Treasury funding restricted in amount and subject to conditions determined by the Secretary of State for the Environment. The Commission agrees a financial memorandum with the Department of the Environment which requires the submission of estimates of expenditure for each forthcoming year. The Commission is required to prepare a statement of account for each financial year for submission to the Secretary of State and, subsequently, the Comptroller and Auditor General. By and large, only limited switching between the main heads of expenditure is permitted. However, the Commission is not required to seek approval for experimental projects and it may alter the balance of expenditure, for example, between grants to the public and private sectors or between grants and promotional work.

The Commission publishes, at least annually, a résumé of its five year rolling programme. This resembles, in some respects, a corporate mission statement which might typically be arranged under the following headings:

- conservation of the countryside;
- promoting enjoyment;
- designated areas;
- promoting awareness and voluntary action;
- special initiatives.

As the rolling programme evolves, inevitably, specific proposals become implemented, modified, extended into other areas or become superseded by other priorities. For example, 'to establish a statutory authority for the Norfolk Broads to be responsible for the conservation and management of the Broads' was an item in the programme of work for 1986/87. The Broads Authority has now been established.

The Commission could not be described as being lavishly funded. Its grant in aid might be considered to be of an order of magnitude commensurate with the amount which a large County Council might allocate to leisure services. By far the largest proportion of this income, of the order of 60%, is disbursed in the form of grants, over two thirds of which goes to public sector organizations. The remaining 40% of its budget is allocated in the following approximate proportions:

60% on staff costs
18% on improving the environmental quality of derelict urban areas under the Operation Groundwork scheme
12% on research
10% on publicity and information.

Owning no land and managing no facilities itself, the Commission attempts to achieve much of its work through partnership with local authorities, public organizations, voluntary bodies and private individuals. Because it is so modestly funded its achievement must be circumscribed. It is difficult, therefore, to evaluate its performance even under the main headings of advice, research, and grant aid. The Commission places primary emphasis on the appearance of the countryside. If there is a conflict between recreation and landscape matters then the landscape issues prevail. The primary thrust of its policies on countryside recreation are largely restricted to facilitating public access to the countryside while its policies on 'conservation' are also focused on landscape conservation. The Commission has a reputation among land managers for seeing countryside management in largely physical terms more akin to landscape maintenance than land management in a broader sense, but this is almost inevitable given the main function of the commission.

2.1.2 National Parks

It is easy to surmise that the National Parks are all under public ownership. This is true in most other countries but not so in England and Wales. They were created to protect certain specific areas of especial beauty and interest, where pressures for a variety of uses (including recreation) were great. The ownership structure within the parks was untouched and no additional public rights were created; consequently, little land is owned by the National Park Authorities of England and Wales. Nevertheless, they do exercise considerable control over the use and development of land and buildings within the designated areas of the Parks. They also provide information on facilities and activities within the area.

The National Parks of England and Wales owe their original formation to the determination and vigour of the outdoor recreation and landscape conservation lobbies and the particular efforts of a number of influential people within them. All of this culminated in the National Parks and Access to the Countryside Act, 1949 which paved the way for the designation and establishment of the present National Parks. Original intentions that they should be administered by autonomous planning boards were only realized in the first two to be designated, namely in the Peak District and the Lake District. For the remainder this model was diluted as a result of lobbying of central government by the constituent local authorities. The County Councils, within whose administrative areas the designated areas fell, assumed control of all subsequent National Parks.

In 1971 the National Parks Review Committee was established to evaluate the extent to which National Parks fulfilled their intended purpose and to make recommendations on future policies. Their recommendations were the subject of Department of the Environment Circular 4176 which indicated that special emphasis was to be given to the following matters.

- Nature conservation, including the encouragement of county councils to establish local nature reserves.
- The encouragement of management agreements between the National Park Authorities and local landowners and the exercise of powers of compulsory acquisition where this was warranted.
- Improved co-ordination of agriculture and other land uses and an extension of the scope of development control to cover the siting of agricultural buildings as well as design and materials.
- Agreement in principle to the notion that forestry operations should be brought within planning control.
- No immediate acceptance of a prohibition on the winning of minerals in National Park areas.
- In considering the siting of a new reservoir, recreational potential to be taken into account.
- Acceptance that there should be a comprehensive and co-ordinated policy for dealing with the social and economic problems of particular areas by means appropriate to the environmental quality of the parks.
- Policies for recreational uses of the parks to be related to the physical characteristics of the area. (This does not, of course, prevent market orientated rather than resource orientated criteria from applying outside the boundary of the designated area, using the park itself as a marketing 'backdrop' to commercial facilities on the fringe of any park.)
- The encouragement of proper management and staffing of recreational facilities within the parks.

The present position is that each National Park is the responsibility of a single National Park Authority advised by a National Park Officer who is in charge of an independent staff. The duties of the park authorities may be classified under three broad headings, namely:

- planning;
- implementation;
- control.

The planning function of the Peak Park Planning Board is significantly greater than any other of the National Park Authorities. It is, for example, the only one with a sole responsibility for producing a structure plan (under the Town and Country Planning Act, 1972) which has more strategic importance than other National Park plans. From this greater overall responsibility stems a more extensive and positive approach to the planning and management of the Peak Park – its resources, inhabitants and visitors – than is yet found elsewhere.

2.1.3 England and Wales Tourist Board

The tourist boards were established under the Development of Tourism Act, 1969 with the objective of encouraging people to visit Britain and encouraging the British to take their holidays in Britain. The English Tourist Board forms the focus of a federation of twelve regional tourist boards. It describes its role as a catalyst: to stimulate private sector investment; to co-ordinate the diverse interests of industry; and to develop and strengthen its marketing. The Wales Tourist Board works in conjunction with three regional tourism councils. The national boards work closely with the regional boards in undertaking their development role. The regional boards provide the link with local authorities and local tourist operators. The national boards formulate policy and co-ordinate research, on a national scale, normally concerned with patterns of participation and expenditure. However, possibly the most important role from a recreational land use point of view is a responsibility to stimulate the provision and improvement of tourism amenities and facilities. This is achieved by:

- providing direct financial and marketing assistance under section 4 of the 1969 Act;
- advice and guidance to organizations with an interest in tourism;
- advice to central government on its tourism policies.

2.2 LOCAL AUTHORITY PROVISION

There is no doubt that the most influential role in local recreation provision is played by local authorities; particularly district and county authorities. However, the nature and extent of provision varies between them; some view the statutory powers which exist for the provision of recreation as an opportunity to be exploited, yet others relegate recreation provision to the level of the non-essential, ignoring the demands for recreation and the exploitation of suitable resources. One of the major obstacles to achieving any uniformity of provision at the local level is that the consumption or enjoyment of leisure facilities cannot, usually, be restricted to the local administrative boundaries which dictate who provides the facilities. This, of course, is simply a recipe for inertia.

In terms of area, the most significant type of leisure provision by the public sector is countryside recreation; followed by outdoor recreation (parks and gardens, usually in urban areas). Countryside and other outdoor facilities are invariably run in-hand by the providing authority (often with financial support from grant-awarding bodies such as the Countryside Commission). The level of investment in staffing, buildings, plant and equipment is low compared with that associated with leisure provision in urban areas.

Area for area the financial site value of built facilities in the urban environment far outweighs that of rural sites. There is, moreover, a strong tradition of local authorities developing and operating their own sports facilities, particularly municipal swimming pools. However, the increase in oil prices during the mid-1970s generated a substantial increase in the running costs of built facilities. The size of the subsequent budgetary deficits, occurring at a time of financial stringency in local authority finance, stimulated local authority interest in cost management to a degree hitherto barely contemplated in the public sector. Meanwhile, as more people (encouraged, in part, by the Sports Councils 'Sport for All' campaign) began to take an active part in sport and leisure, it became evident that they were prepared to travel to find their choice of recreation. This broader participating public was less ready to accept the over-regimented view of leisure provision traditionally characterized by the public sector. They were prepared to look elsewhere if their new tastes are not accommodated locally. This trend stimulated greater appreciation of the importance of market-led management in modern recreation provision by the public sector.

Faced with these new pressures and demands, the public sector has become much readier to enlist the help of the private sector on a partnership basis. It is not uncommon these days to find leisure facilities provided by the public sector but operated entirely, or in part, by the private sector. Similarly it is no longer exceptional to find commercial sponsorship being given a place in public sector leisure provision. In relatively exceptional circumstances it is possible to find instances where the public sector has simply provided a site for leisure development and encouraged the private sector to develop and operate the appropriate facility.

Local Planning Authorities are empowered under sections 7, 8, 9 and 10 of the Countryside Act, 1968 to provide facilities and carry out works in country parks, on common land and on camping and picnic sites. They may, for example, erect buildings; carry out site works; provide car park areas; or provide facilities for sailing, boating, fishing and bathing. If the land in question does not belong to them, they may carry out works in agreement with the owners. They also have powers of compulsory acquisition if these are needed to enable them to carry out their functions under the Act. It should be pointed out, however, that these powers are viewed as being of great political sensitivity.

These powers apply to county and district authorities and consultation should occur between them; indeed, a district authority may require the consent of the appropriate county authority to implement proposals under the Act. It is clear from our enquiries that the Act has been implemented in different ways in different parts of the country. In some cases a County Council has taken the initiative and has established and run countryside recreational facilities and in doing so has taken on the planning and subsequent management function. A good example of this is Hampshire County

Council. In other cases a County Council may see itself as having a responsibility to advise district councils on the implementation of the Act but without becoming involved in detailed initiation or subsequent management. There are, of course, arrangements between these two extremes but in all cases the arrangements are mutable as people, politics and finances alter.

Each county is, in one respect or other, different from every other. Different in setting; in its countryside; in the degree of urbanization within and beyond its boundaries; and different, therefore, in its real or apparent attractiveness to the day visitor or long-term holiday-maker. Some County Councils, particularly those administering an area subject to a keen demand for recreation, have special departments with titles such as 'Recreation' or 'Leisure Services' or 'Countryside and Recreation' the officers of which are charged with the responsibility for initiating and managing recreational facilities which may include art galleries, museums, libraries, footpaths and picnic sites as well as more conventional countryside recreation. Elsewhere, recreational provision may be added to the responsibilities of other departments such as 'Planning', 'Estates' or 'Highways'. The organization of leisure services in the late 1960s and early 1970s, when the leisure explosion of that era occurred, appears to have depended largely on the assessment of need and, perhaps, the enthusiasm of the Council's officers and elected representatives. Time and experience sometimes change initial perceptions while financial constraints sometimes change priorities and by the late 1980s some enthusiastically created posts have disappeared while in other cases an extension of management involvement has been warranted. As the demand for recreation ebbs and flows across the country, regardless of administrative boundaries, so the need for recreation provision and management will also change.

Not all County Councils have a separate recreation department. In such cases it is common practice for the planning department to take primary responsibility for countryside recreation provision while the estates department is usually responsible for developing and managing facilities provided by the council. Some counties have the additional organizational complication of having to accommodate all or part of a National Park (separately administered) within their boundary. Others may have to contend with specific pressures generated as a result of their natural landscape. Those bordering the sea have to contend with the special pressures of the holiday-maker along the maritime fringe on fine days in the season (and in the interior in dismal weather). Counties which are tourist destinations are faced with the problem of providing for thousands of visitors from outside their borders in addition to the requirements of their own inhabitants for both recreation and protection of the countryside and coast. Recreation for the indigenous population is not necessarily significantly different from that required by the visitors while protection of the environment should balance control against the economic benefit which is capable of being generated by recreation and tourism. Counties not subject to undue recreational pressure see the emphasis of their countryside policies more as conserving and protecting the countryside.

A difficulty which is endemic in the field of recreation provision both in the public and in the private sectors is that of assessing and evaluating demand. Whatever the public wants or needs has to be expressed in terms which are appropriate for the detailed design and specification of facilities which could best meet that demand. Not only will this govern what is to be provided but also how much is to be provided. This aspect of policy formulation must give most concern to officers in the public sector charged with the initiation and management of leisure facilities in the countryside, for it is on the assessment of likely demand that site selection and design are normally based. If that assessment is wrong there is a consequent danger of creating facilities which are under-used and expensive to run (per capita of visitors) or, conversely, facilities which have inadequate capacity to cope with demand.

Policy making is an important function of a local authority and it is usually exercised through the appropriate committee or subcommittee of the elected representatives of the council acting on the advice of the professional officers servicing that committee. Most County Councils have something akin to a Recreation and Leisure Committee or Countryside Committee or similarly titled subcommittees. They may have a rather narrow recreational brief or may be charged with recommending action to the council on a whole range of matters such as countryside conservation, recreation and leisure, trees and woodlands, wildlife, footpaths, interpretation and information services. These committees are serviced and advised by the appropriate officers of the council departments concerned such as planning, estates, education, highways and, of course, recreation.

Although the emphasis of the last few paragraphs has been on the provision of facilities, the public sector also plays an important role in influencing private sector provision through the development control process. Development control policies are determined by the broad planning policies of the county or district planning authority. These policies are contained in a variety of planning documents prepared and issued by the relevant planning authorities, which must be interpreted against the background of legislation and circulars from central government. Strategic issues of the type associated with structure plans identify the source and nature of the trends underlying more detailed policy formulation. By referring to the Structure Plan and related information, the land manager is better able to foresee those areas of his or her function most likely to be constrained by development control and also opportunities which may otherwise have been obscure or speculative which may warrant further investigation. Irrespective of whether or not land managers are able to benefit from this broader view of the planning policy they must each work within, or at least alongside, those planning policies which relate to their areas of operation. This can be a source of much frustration. The development of recreation enterprises in the countryside normally requires consent from the planning authority for a change of use from, typically, agriculture or forestry; it may place demands on the physical infrastructure of rural areas for which they are ill-equipped; it may involve the development of buildings and ancillary facilities which are out of keeping with the character of the area.

It would be comforting to believe that recreation provision by either sector followed the kind of rational and systematic procedure designed to 'optimize' provision in the light of the prevailing demand. Unfortunately the reality is not as tidy as this. Private developers are likely to look carefully for the 'best' site to maximize demand provided they are confident that the demand is sufficiently effective to maintain a commitment to pay for the facilities they provide. While the public sector is unlikely to be looking for the same commercial commitment, financial constraints as much as anything else are likely to mean that provision is determined largely by opportunity (which may have little in common with the land use strategy in the local or structure plan). In the case of provision, therefore, development control may encourage private developers to look for appropriate sites by planning permission being refused on inappropriate sites. Conversely, a local authority, seeking to exploit an unplanned opportunity may be able to convince its own planning committee that otherwise prohibitive policies should be relaxed for the social benefits which the opportunity may offer. Further justification for this may stem from the relative commitment of the respective developers to the completed facility. The private developer will be motivated to maintain the facility solely because of commercial commitment to it; the public developer is more likely to be motivated by social commitment, which may be less transient than its commercial equivalent.

Countryside and recreation policy-planning is an early step in the process of implementing and maintaining recreational land uses. However, success or failure will be judged by the physical manifestation which follows. Few if any facilities run themselves. Even at the most basic level of countryside provision, a wardening, scavenging and maintenance service must be provided. In many instances the latter two functions used to be carried out by, or with the assistance of, the local district council. Sometimes the repair and maintenance of equipment such as services, fences, gates, and car park facilities were undertaken by an itinerant maintenance staff under the control of the appropriate County Council. Country parks of sufficient size often have their own repair staff but recreation departments may have to beg or borrow staff from others; for example, some rurally based councils have, in the past, had a forestry officer with a permanent staff of woodmen able to provide useful assistance with site maintenance. Many of these 'routine' services must now be offered for competitive tendering and are now just as likely, therefore, to be undertaken by private contractors.

All facilities need to be monitored for signs of physical deterioration and many also need monitoring to ensure that they are being used in the intended manner (and it may be, of course, that the 'intended manner changes over time'). This is sometimes done passively by providing visitor information or interpretation centres designed to present the site to visitors, orientate them and explain how the site should be used to its best advantage. These centres are sometimes staffed and there is little doubt that visitors like to be able to refer to someone who 'belongs' to the site for guidance and information. This is a role which frequently falls to wardens or rangers who tend to spend their time out in the field rather than indoors.

Wardening is a service which has evolved alongside the provision of country parks and open space. The countryside warden is a person whose professional parentage extends from the park-keeper through gamekeeper, botanist, entomologist, ornithologist, walker, mountaineer and skirting narrowly around police officer. The warden is a very special person who understands the countryside and whose duties may range from the professional on-site manager to the ranger-warden-maintenance person. Most importantly, a warden must understand how to deal with people as various as the knowledgeably inquisitive walker; the irritably frustrated caravanner; the truculent and tiresome visitor with little apparent interest in the place being visited. A chief warden may be the site manager or may simply be in charge of a wardening staff.

It is common practice to provide a warden or ranger with a uniform which is readily identifiable to the general public but which also creates a degree of officialdom which the public is, in the main, prepared to accept and respect. The style of uniform may be important in denoting the function of the wearers and, indeed, their likely knowledge and attitude. In country parks near large towns a warden may have to deal with people whose attitude may be aggressive and whose knowledge of the countryside is limited. On the other hand, countryside patrolled by rangers in dark blue uniforms with alsatians at their heels rather spoils the impression that the area is to be used for quiet enjoyment and peaceful exercise.

It is not easy to make adequate provision for the needs and tastes of everyone, nor is it always possible to find the money to do so. In times of financial stringency countryside recreation has, in many cases, to take a lowly place on the list of priorities. Most local authorities are, understandably, careful about making admission charges, particularly to their countryside facilities. As a general rule, they are ready to levy an admission charge to contribute to the day to day running of the facility but seldom to cover the major fixed costs of provision such as the loan charges attributable to the capital costs; or the rent charge attributable to the land; or the administrative/departmental costs attributable to the council's overall provision.

There was a time when publicly provided recreational facilities were either unpriced or where charges were very low. This gave rise to the accusation from the private sector of unfair competition. However, it is now common practice for local authorities to levy a charge for specific facilities where a charge:

- can easily be made;
- is readily accepted by the users;
- costs less to collect than is obtained in receipts.

Such charges would cover fishing and boating or the use of caravan and camping sites and, quite often, car parking. It may well be that this tendency to charge for specific facilities will increase partly because the public gets used to the idea of having to pay, partly because the authority feels that there must be a limit to the unrecoverable expenditure which can be met annually out of public funds, and partly because the number of special attractions provided in out of town locations will increase. However, this type of pricing differs from the increasingly common practice in the private sector of making one admission charge which includes all facilities within the site.

The 1970s saw a boom in expenditure on public recreation facilities. In urban areas this boom manifested itself in the construction of many large, purpose built sports centres some of which are now seen as being inappropriate for local demands and expensive to run and maintain. In the countryside the vogue for country parks produced many which are inconveniently located in relation to the urban population and too dull and contrived to appeal to those already living in the countryside. If and when finance again becomes more readily available, it is reasonable to expect that councils and their advisers, being now more knowledgeable on the subject of recreation, will tend to concentrate on developing areas already in hand and confining new recreational ventures to suitable sites on the urban fringe. Facilities could be more flexible and adaptable in use, accommodating, for example a better mix of sport, education, leisure and relaxation. Countryside interpretation on urban fringe sites using indoor exhibitions rather than nature trails or guided walks offers the bonus of a building which could be put to different uses at different times of the year.

As management knowledge and expertise improve most authorities are now producing management plans both for new areas brought into use and existing areas for which there is no explicit plan. The form and content of management plans will be tailored to meet the requirements of the operating authority. However, some so-called management plans are little more than a summary of ideas in the form of a site layout. This is totally inadequate for management purposes. In the provision of countryside recreation the Countryside Commission has consistently pressed local authorities to produce management plans for their countryside facilities (making this a condition of grant aid) but until the publication of *Management Plans (A guide to their preparation and use)* in 1986, was itself ill equipped to give sound guidance on the preparation of a good plan.

This highlights a fairly widespread dilemma in recreation provision, namely the nature of the boundary between recreation planning and the subsequent development and management of a site. Within a local authority, the planning department needs to be centrally involved in the earliest stages of planning recreational provision to determine social and physical priorities (e.g. consideration of the type of facility which should be provided, for whom and where). The management orientated staff of the corresponding recreation department might argue that there are many practical facets to these questions for which planners are ill equipped to provide the best answers. In the end, the right answer is surely that there is no exact boundary between the functions of the two departments. Any development planned without management considerations being incorporated at the very beginning is likely to lead to ineffective and inefficient facilities but, equally, any site must be considered in a broad context. Nevertheless, once the need, type, function and location of a recreational area has been determined the functional design of the site is more properly the province of those equipped to ensure that the site functions in the best possible way.

FURTHER READING

Rogers, A., Blundel, J. and Curry, N. (eds.) (1985) *The Countryside Handbook*, Croom Helm, London.

Leay, M. J., Rowe, J. and Young, J. D. (1986) *Management Plans (A guide to their preparation and use)*, Countryside Commission, Cheltenham.

<table>
<tr><td>**3**</td><td># Management and the legal environment</td></tr>
</table>

3.1 INTRODUCTION

Organizing and being organized are axiomatic of management. The purpose of management is to achieve, by organized action, a better use of resources than would otherwise have occurred in the natural course of events. The extent to which this is achieved will depend partly on how well the management organization functions in making, taking and implementing decisions. Although its form and way of operating may be largely a matter for self-determination, the decisions which are made and the way in which they are implemented will have an effect on the world at large. There are numerous controls over and sanctions against the unreasonable actions of organizations and individuals which are not self-determined but are contained within 'the law of the land'. The influence of the law extends to the economic and social relations which exist within the unit and, moreover, the physical conditions within the organization. This chapter is intended to explore, in broad terms, the influence of the law on the use and management of land for recreation.

Management organizations function in a broad social and economic context created by the collective actions of all members of the community. They need to be responsive to this societal context without necessarily being subject to any specific influence of individual members of the public. Thus, the law influences the relationship between an organization and the world at large and also the relationships within the organization itself. Figure 3.1 represents the management organization encircled by a set of 'collars' which constrain the uninhibited actions of management organizations.

One of those collars of constraint represents the legal milieu within which management organizations must function and sometimes referred to as the external management environment. By implication there is a corresponding internal environment which governs the way in which individuals behave in relation to their organization and to each other. The law also

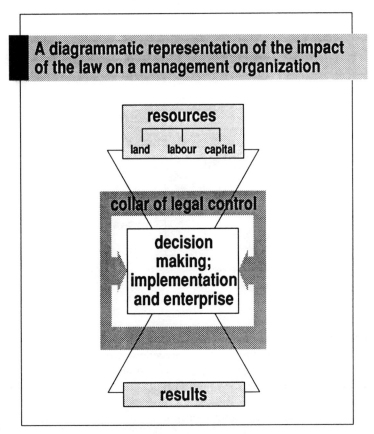

Fig. 3.1 A diagrammatic representation of the impact of the law on a management organization.

extends to this internal environment. In view of the fact that the law is capable of extending its influence into virtually every aspect of management it is reasonable to enquire by what authority this influence is exercised. As the significance of international, particularly European, law increases the answer to this enquiry becomes increasingly involved. However, to keep the present discussion as simple as possible, the two most important domestic sources of legal power may be singled out. These are English Common Law and Statute.

3.2 SOURCES OF LEGAL AUTHORITY

The English Common Law has been evolved by the Courts of Justice since time immemorial. This is not the place to delve into the historical

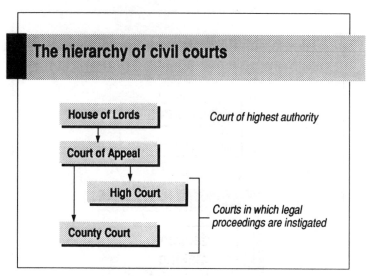

Fig. 3.2 Hierarchy of courts.

development of Common Law, it is enough to say that it is essentially judge-made, based on the principle of precedence. A body of 'legal wisdom' has been accumulated over centuries by judges hearing and recording actual disputes brought before the courts for arbitration and judgement. This body of wisdom is vast but is classified into some order of priority by treating judgements from some courts as being more important than the judgements from others. The courts of England and Wales form a hierarchy of authority, as illustrated in Figure 3.2, with the House of Lords as the court of highest authority. Thus, decisions of the House of Lords are binding on all other courts while decisions from courts lower down the hierarchy are binding on those lower still, sometimes with a right of appeal to the next level up.

The authority of judges to 'make new law' seldom extends beyond their power to interpret the facts contained in the cases they hear. Parliament has no such restriction; it has the authority of being the supreme governing body of the country elected by the enfranchised population. New laws are introduced, debated and decided by simple majority of the Houses of Parliament or their committees. Acts of Parliament prescribe the law of the land directly and indirectly by subsidiary forms of legislation which include statutory instruments, bylaws, government white paper and circulars. Normally the statutes themselves provide for their own implementation but matters arising from a failure to comply with the law are dealt with by the courts. They also administer the penalties and sanctions precipitated if the law is transgressed.

3.3 CIVIL AND CRIMINAL LAW CONTRASTED

It is important at this point to distinguish between criminal and civil law, for, among other things, the respective remedies differ. A crime is a wrong perpetrated against a member of society and, as such, considered to be an affront to society as a whole. The object of a criminal action is to punish anyone found guilty beyond all reasonable doubt of a criminal act; compensating the victim is of secondary importance. Civil law is concerned with the settlement of disputes between individuals. The primary object of a civil action is to restore, on a balance of probability considering the facts of the case, the proper balance of equity between the parties to a dispute (usually, though not always, by financial compensation or 'damages'); punishing the wrongdoer is of secondary importance.

It requires a certain amount of determination on the part of a law-abiding citizen to become a criminal and it is relatively unusual to find management organizations being involved in criminal actions. As a general rule, a guilty act requires a guilty mind; motive and criminal intent are usually required; mere ineptitude is seldom enough. Consequently, little further reference will be made to criminal law; it is best avoided at all costs. On the other hand, the damages and other penalties associated with civil actions may be considered by the cavalier manager to be something of an occupational hazard and an unfortunate cost of production. It should be remembered, however, that failure to comply with a judgement in a civil case may be viewed by the courts as contempt of the court, a criminal offence attracting appropriate punishment until the contempt is purged by complying with the original judgement. The legal tapestry into which the operational life of most organizations is woven may be extremely elaborate. The volume of published material is immense so it is only possible here to point out some of the salient threads by way of illustration. These will consist of law relating to land and land tenure; commercial contracts; general civil wrongs; corporate structure; environmental control.

3.4 THE LAW RELATING TO LAND AND LAND TENURE

Land is a fundamental component of recreational land management and the law relating to the land is an appropriate starting point. It is important to understand that, as a general principle, there is no general right available to the general public in England and Wales giving a right of access to land. Like it or not (and there are some who manifestly do not), English law has, over centuries, evolved a system of private land ownership as distinct from a system of public domain. It should be noted, however, that public or corporate bodies may be entitled to the same rights of ownership as any individual member of the public.

Ever since William the Conqueror expropriated the land of his Saxon predecessors, no one other than 'the Crown', has had absolute ownership of the land itself. Rights to the use of land are all that can be 'owned'. The closest it is possible to come to absolute ownership of land is to possess, in perpetuity, the right to freedom of use of the land in question. This entitlement is called 'a fee simple absolute in possession' but more commonly referred to as a freehold estate or freehold ownership. It only applies, of course, to a specific, clearly defined area of land, hence the common misconception that an 'estate' is an area of land when it more correctly describes the legal right to freedom of use in perpetuity of the land.

A freehold estate can be assigned to someone else who then becomes the new 'owner'. The assignment can relate to all or just part of the land which was covered by the original freehold. Thus, freehold estates can be divided or assembled in many permutations. Furthermore, the package of rights which the freehold represents can also be dismantled. For example, a freeholder may give up the right to occupy the property for, say, seven years to another person by granting them a lease in return for a rent for the seven years. When the lease expires the freeholder is entitled to resume occupation of the property.

This kind of arrangement introduced the concept of landlord and tenant which takes us into a distinct area of law related to the law of property but combining it with the law of contract. At the beginning of this century, even though 90% of the countryside was tenanted, the landowners exercised almost complete control over its use. The same is not true today; tenants have far greater freedom of management and security of tenure (granted by statute) than their forebears. Landlord and tenant is complex and the danger for the unwary is that a landowner may unwittingly grant a right which was not really intended but which, nevertheless, the courts may uphold. The rights of freeholders or leaseholders are also subject to other rights such as easements (which include rights of way); *profits à prendre* (which include common rights) and restrictive covenants.

Returning to the issue of public access to the countryside, the entitlement to use land or even gain access to it belongs to the owner of the legal estate in that land (namely the freehold or leasehold owner) who is entitled to exclusive and quiet (namely undisturbed) enjoyment of the property. This entitlement is protected by the law of trespass to property, unusual in that, unlike other civil wrong-doings it is actionable without proof of damage. This benefit can be shared with others, of course, but, as a general rule, not without the explicit or implied consent of the owner. In which case they become licensees.

For any recreation enterprise, it is of paramount importance that the operator occupies the property on terms which allow the use to be exercised. In the case of agricultural tenants, for example, their lease will entitle them to occupy the farm for the purposes of farming but is likely to preclude any non-agricultural use such as recreation. The benefit of rights of use and occupation other than the freehold, is likely to give rise to a financial charge – a rent. Indeed, the financial value of any piece of land is always tied to the legal interest which gives rise to the entitlement to use the property. A landlord traditionally takes no part in the risk of the enterprise, but merely provides the operator with an opportunity to run the enterprise in return for a rent. The capital value of the rent is inversely proportional to the risk associated with its security and prospects for growth. Generally speaking, the risk associated with commercially operated recreation enterprises is high.

On broad matters of land use, statutory controls now restrict the freedom of owners or occupiers to move land out of one use and into another, from agriculture to recreation, for example. We should remember, however, that despite the danger of abuse inherent in the great freedom which landowners once enjoyed, many of the landscape legacies which we now seek passionately to protect were the result of their prerogative action.

3.5 THE LAW RELATING TO CONTRACTUAL RELATIONS

Another area of law with which most managers live cheek by jowl is that governing contractual relations (which forms part of a large body of law governing commercial relations). There are seven essential requirements for a contract to be sufficiently valid for it to be enforced by the courts. They are as follows:

- there must be an offer;
- there must be acceptance of that offer;
- the contract must be in the correct form whether that be oral, in writing or by deed;
- there must be consideration for the subject of the offer;
- there must be an intention to be bound by the contract;
- the parties to the contract must have legal capacity to be party to it, so, for example, the law will not recognize children as parties to a contract;
- a contract for an inherently illegal purpose is void.

Even an action as apparently straightforward as buying goods from a shop may not be as obvious as it appears at first sight. The goods on display are not on offer, they constitute 'an invitation to treat'. The customer offers to purchase the goods. This offer is normally accepted by the shopkeeper and the consideration for the goods is the purchase price. The offer may have some implied terms such as an assumption that the goods are what they seem and fit for the purpose for which they are intended; indeed, much of the consumer protection legislation is based on support for such reasonably implied terms.

If a person enters into a valid contract then breaches its terms, the injured party or parties may bring an action in the courts (i.e. sue) for damages to repair the injury they have suffered, or may ask the courts to insist that the terms of the contract be properly performed. The full ramifications of the law governing contractual relations are extensive but this summary may illustrate the kind of legal sequence of events which commercial transactions can set in train.

The evolution of English company law played a significant role in the encouragement of the corporate company structure. This in turn had a significant effect in relation to the matter of legal capacity to be bound by the terms of a contract. The case of *Salamon* v. *Salamon and Company Ltd.* (1897) established the principle that the personality of a company can exist separately from the individual personalities of the shareholders who own it. There is, in other words, a veil between a company and its shareholders. In considering the actions of a company the law will not, as a general rule, look behind the veil. Thus, in the case of a limited company, the shareholders are only liable to share the losses of the company to the extent of their actual share holding. In contrast, partnerships do not usually attract similar treatment. The partners share the profits and losses equally (unless there is a partnership agreement which says otherwise) and are individually liable for any losses which the partnership may suffer.

3.6 THE LAW OF TORT

One of the most formidable and far-reaching areas of civil law dates back to the Normans and is called the law of tort (tort being the Norman–French word for 'wrong'). It is a collective term which embraces numerous separately named torts. Some of the names are quite familiar, the torts of libel and slander for example, while others such as false imprisonment are more remote. Several torts have special relevance to land management including:

- trespass to property;
- occupier's liability to third parties;
- nuisance;
- liability for the storage of dangerous substances;
- negligence.

The last of these is in many ways the most far-reaching tort of all. It is concerned with the common duty of care we all owe to our fellow human beings. Not only does the law of negligence recognize this duty of care, it provides that if we negligently breach that duty and, as a consequence, damage results, then we may be held liable in damages for all the loss which can reasonably be said to have resulted from the breach. The courts will consider the extent of the duty of care owing in any given circumstance. So, when negligence occurs as a result of ineptitude on the part of an individual or organization acting in a professional capacity, the remedial reproach of the court is likely to be expressed in stark financial terms.

3.7 STATUTE

Many areas of common law have become the subject of statute and in some respects this simplifies ancient and complex case law. However, the influence of statute extends well beyond the confines of common law. Where common law has been too slow to respond to areas of rapid change detrimental to society as a whole (for example, environmental pollution) Parliament may see fit to step in and create new law. It is not uncommon to find such legislation prescribing sanctions and punishments if its terms are disobeyed. The volume of legislation now on the statute book is so great that there is little point in singling out specific examples. It is probably sufficient to say that in any and all of the areas in which management plays any part there is sure to be a body of relevant legislation.

It is part of the discipline of any manager to be attuned to the whole complex web of the law and to be aware of the general field of legislation relevant to his or her area of concern. There is a legal maxim that ignorance is no excuse in the eyes of the law. All managers must, therefore, be able to identify when proper legal advice is required. If it is called on too soon solicitors fees will add unnecessarily to the overall costs of management. If it is called on too late even greater costs are likely to accrue in court and lawyers costs. The safety net under this particular management tight-rope could be indemnity insurance so that the costs of a fall may at least be cushioned. What is sure is that no modern manager can afford to ignore the impact of the law.

The most notable characteristic of the postwar development of the law relating to land management is the proliferation of statutory rules. These embrace:

- land use planning and environmental control;
- tenure of property;
- fiscal policy (i.e. local and national taxation).

Land use planning and environmental control includes development control; building regulations; control of pollution; conservation. Management includes employment legislation; visitor protection; operating licences; management agreements.

3.8 LAND USE PLANNING AND ENVIRONMENTAL CONTROL

One of the most typical aspects of the control of building development in the countryside was introduced by the Green Belt (London and Home Counties) Act, 1938. The geographical definition of the 'Green Belt' has been considerably extended since 1938 but the original concept that there should be a rural *cordon sanitaire* preventing the expansion of urban areas (originally the metropolis) remains every bit as pertinent today. It is not easy, however, to reconcile the very strong presumption against development of any kind in green belt areas with the mounting demand for recreational facilities to be provided in the so-called urban fringe (which may be viewed, conversely, as the rural fringe).

Comprehensive land use planning was first introduced in this country by the Town and Country Planning Act, 1947 which introduced the concept of a development 'blueprint' for town and country in the form of 'development plans'. The 1947 Act also represented a milestone in controlling all new development other than as a simple adjunct to the existing public health legislation. Virtually any form of land use was defined as 'development' for the purposes of the Act and all development required consent from the local planning authority. Consent could be refused, granted or granted subject to conditions and an enforcement procedure gave local planning authorities the power to ensure that this development control was observed.

However, in order to make the system less cumbersome and pedantic, the legislation introduced certain categories of development for which planning consent was normally deemed to be granted.

1. A General Development Order introduced 23 cases of deemed consent which included agricultural and forestry uses and temporary uses enduring for no more than 28 days each year.
2. A Use Class Order which groups together broadly similar uses into a number of categories (currently 18).

Despite the fact that a change of land use normally constitutes development for the purposes of the legislation, change of use within a 'use class' does not require planning consent. The 'permitted development' provisions, which constitute an important concession within agriculture and forestry, do not apply in those parts of the country designated as a National Park or Area of Outstanding Natural Beauty (AONB) under the National Parks and Access to the Countryside Act, 1949.

If planning can be thought of as the art of making rational decisions, then land use planners employed by local planning authorities apply their skills to achieve a rational and effective arrangement of land uses. This arrangement is expressed in planning documents available for public scrutiny. The land use arrangement favoured by any planning authority must be achieved either through the development control process (which is essentially negative in nature) or by the direct acquisition of ownership rights (essentially positive in nature) for the positive power of implementation, and subsequent management still rests with the owner or occupier of a site.

3.9 ACCESS

One area of countryside management which remains a constant focus for debate and discussion is that of public access to the countryside. This debate extends to demands for landowners to forgo their power to prohibit public entry onto their land. Discounting the Access to the Mountains Act, 1939, which was never implemented, the first piece of legislation which dealt with public access to the countryside in a comprehensive manner was the National Parks and Access to the Countryside Act, 1949. Part V of this Act was devoted to the provision of access to open country (including mountain, moor, heath, down, cliff or foreshore) by access agreements or access orders. Access agreements could be entered into by a local authority and landowners in the area and in the event of failure to reach agreement an access order could be made.

The provisions of the 1949 Act were also extended by the Countryside Act, 1968. In particular the 1968 Act enabled local planning authorities to set up and equip country parks and picnic sites and to make bylaws to control their use. It also recognized the role which the motor car was increasingly playing in enabling and encouraging the public to enjoy the countryside by allowing special provision to be made for car parking and for the control of vehicular traffic in the countryside.

The idea of agreements between local authorities and private landowners to secure the social benefit of access was extended even further by the Wildlife and Countryside Act, 1981 to the broader concept of management of the countryside for other than short term commercial objectives. The 1981 Act enabled local authorities to enter into management agreements with landowners for the purposes of enhancing the amenity or natural beauty of the countryside, essentially to prevent sensitive areas of the countryside from being damaged by modern farming practice.

Returning more directly to the subject of access to the countryside for informal recreation, the organization which has probably played the most siginificant role in providing public access to attractive countryside and coast is the National Trust for England and Wales (Scotland and Northern Ireland have their own). The Trust is a private organization and, in the main, secures access by acquiring land and property for this express purpose. It was first established in 1894 and made a body corporate by private act of parliament entitled the National Trust Act, 1907. The Trust is now estimated to own in the region of 600 square miles of land and water and to be tenant of a further 30 square miles.

The example of the National Trust highlights a legal dilemma which the issue of access raises. The Trust is able to grant access expressly within its powers as a landowner. The English law of property is founded on the principle of private rights to the exclusion of public rights and the history of land ownership has moved progressively further in this direction since 1066. Access and management agreements essentially amount to a purchase of rights of access from landowners but unless access can be granted through ownership of the land in question or by acquiring specific rights then, apart from public rights of way, urban commons and the coastal strip between high and low water mark in most places, there is no right of public domain and, in the absence of the permission of the landowner, the public have no right of access, subject to the Rights of Way Act, 1990, onto land in England and Wales. This does not apply to anything like the same extent to the countryside of Scotland.

By the same token, if a landowner or occupier does permit visitors to enter onto that estate by express or implied authority (anyone else being a trespasser) then the landowner or occupier owes a duty of care, now enshrined in the Occupiers Liability Act, 1957, to those visitors. Section 2 of the Act defines the duty of care as 'a duty to take such care as in all the circumstances of the case is reasonable to see that visitors will be reasonably safe in using the premises for the purpose of which they are permitted by the occupier to be there'. The occupier will normally be expected to have greater knowledge of the condition of the premises than others and should, therefore, be in the best position to guard against the dangers which may arise from them. Warning against possible dangers will only reduce the responsibility of the occupier if, in all the circumstances, that warning is effective enough to enable visitors taking reasonable care to avoid the danger.

A person who in the normal course of events enters premises as a visitor but continues to parts of the premises where entry is forbidden then becomes a trespasser. The duty of care owed to a trespasser is less onerous on the occupier than that owed to a visitor and the 1957 Act does not apply to trespassers. The occupier must have acted with total disregard for the existence of a trespasser before failing in what amounts to the simplest humanitarian duty of care. As well as not applying to trespassers, the 1957 Act does not apply to visitors to the countryside who are there by virtue of the National Parks and Access to the Countryside Act, 1949. They will only benefit, therefore, from the duty of care owed to trespassers.

The degree of reasonableness in taking care to avoid danger will vary between classes of visitor and the circumstances under which they enter the premises. Adults, for example, may reasonably be assumed to guard against any risks reasonably inherent in their being on the premises whereas children may be assumed to be inherently less careful. Where visitors enter premises under a contract with the intention of using those premises, the common duty of care may still apply in circumstances not directly covered by the contract, provided they have not, in the meantime, become trespassers.

Any manager may be conversant with the legal framework within which the organization operates but inevitably must rely on other members of the organization whose knowledge may be less complete. In a recreation facility this applies in particular to employees to whom responsibility for the day to day operation of the facility is delegated and who probably have most face to face contact with the public. If an employee by act or omission transgresses the law, on the employer's behalf as it were, who is liable, employee or employer? In the light of modern employment relationships the courts may adopt various criteria in answering this question. The general rule is that an employer will be responsible for acts or omissions committed by employees in the course of their employment (i.e. within the class of acts they are employed to do or as a necessary incident to that employment) and resulting in damage to third parties.

The general burden of this liability may be contrasted, however, with that arising from an independent contractor (as distinct from an employee) employed for a specific, finite purpose. In general an employer will not be liable for the acts or omissions of an independent contractor committed in the course of the work the contractor is employed to do. The position of concessionaires in this web of responsibilities is less clear-cut, particularly as exceptions to the general rules may prevent the employee from escaping liability. The issue to be borne in mind is whether or not the employer is in breach of his or her own duty rather than the contractor or concessionaire being in breach of theirs. Employers who are also the occupiers of the premises cannot escape the occupier's duty of care by delegating it to a third party; they remain duty bound to see that care is taken. Consequently where the legal occupier of premises operated by a concessionaire invites visitors onto the premises, the occupier must take care to ensure the safety of the premises.

The recreational land manager must also be aware of the employer/employee relationship in a different context. The Health and Safety at Work Act, 1974 (section 2) places a responsibility on employers for securing health, safety and welfare for employees but section 3 also extends this obligation to include 'other persons'. The responsibility for enforcing the Health and Safety Regulations lies with the local authority and in the event of a failure to comply with the provisions of the Act, 'it shall be for the accused to prove that it was not reasonably practicable to do more than was in fact done to satisfy the duty or requirement or that there was no better practicable means than was in fact used to satisfy the duty or requirement' (section 40).

Although the code of law will shape future actions, its controlling function is inevitably retrospective in operation. No matter how certain a manager may be that proper safeguards have been taken for the welfare of visitors, employees and third parties, unforeseen events may occur in the light of which, nevertheless, the courts may view the safeguards as inadequate. The penalty associated with such a judgement may be substantial and the manager would be prudent in indemnifying any liability by taking out appropriate insurance. The matter of indemnification is complex and an area warranting expert advice.

3.10 FISCAL POLICY

Even in countries with the most *laissez-faire* of economic policies, government involves some expenditure. This is partly to fund the cost of the framework of government (the legislature, the executive or civil service and the judicature); partly to maintain order and stability among the population (the police); partly to maintain the security of the country against the danger of external aggression (the armed services); and, in the majority of developed nations of any size, to provide a framework of welfare provision to minimize the effects of social inequality and deprivation. All of this must be paid for and the primary source of revenue is society at large which is taxed in a variety of ways.

At national level tax revenue is the responsibility of the Inland Revenue and of the Customs and Excise. The Inland Revenue is responsible for the collection of tax levied on income and capital receipts. This is known as direct taxation. The Customs and Excise is responsible for the collection of tax levied on the value of goods sold. This is known as indirect taxation. Local authorities also have powers to raise local taxes – in the case of recreational enterprises by means of a tax called 'rates' levied on the value of the property. Thus, in the case of a recreation enterprise employing staff, the impact of taxation will have the following effects. If the enterprise is a company it will be liable for the payment of Corporation Tax on the income generated by the company. Employees and shareholders of the company will be liable for Income Tax on the income which they earn as salaries, wages or dividends. The enterprise will be charged Value Added Tax on all goods and services which are sold, including the cost of admission. (It is normal practice for this to be passed on to the visitors.) If the enterprise sells a capital asset which has increased in value or if the enterprise itself is sold, thereby releasing a capital gain, Capital Gains Tax may be payable.

Most transactions involving an exchange of value are likely to attract taxation of one form or other. The rules governing liability for tax and the quantum of tax to be paid in given circumstances is based almost entirely on statute and the case law which surrounds its interpretation. Taxation represents the clearest interface between commerce and the law. It is relatively unusual in that the responsible bodies may express a view that a liability for tax arises in a certain sum, leaving the target of that assessment to disprove or dispute liability. Taxation is an unproductive cost for any recreational land manager. There are many examples of costs of development, implementation and day to day running being needlessly high because of inadequate forward planning to minimize the impact of the tax liability. There are many examples of operators being caught unawares when a tax bill has materialized, even to the extent of being forced into liquidation. Tax planning is a vital prerequisite for virtually any enterprise.

FURTHER READING

Bonyhady, T. (1987) *The Law of the Countryside*, Professional Books, Abingdon.
Collins, V. (1984) *Recreation and the Law*, E & FN Spon, London.
James, P.S. (1989) *Introduction to English Law*, 12th ed, Butterworths, London.
McAuslan, P. (1975) *Land, Law and Planning*, Weidenfeld and Nicolson, London.

Market analysis and consumer behaviour

There is a degree of inherent ambiguity in this title, for it marks an important threshold between economics and management. Economists tend to be preoccupied with demand as it actually exists and the conditions which have given rise to its manifestation. Managers are also interested in this but must go beyond the point where economists begin to lose confidence, namely, forecasting and acting upon future demand. Patterns and levels of demand which are ostensibly hidden must be made manifest by the decisions which the manager chooses to implement. Managers do not simply react to the wisdom of hindsight, they are proactive; they must create success. Economists may speculate about future demand while enterprising managers must make it happen. In doing so, managers cannot rely on intuition and luck; as a famous golfer once said when told he was a 'lucky' player 'it's funny, the more I practise the luckier I seem to get'. Managers need a proper awareness of their own vulnerability and must appreciate the extent to which they are master or mistress of their own destiny.

4.1 'PRODUCT' DEFINITION – THE RECREATION EXPERIENCE

In some respects the demand requirements associated with recreation in the countryside are more particular than for any other rural land use. We are not dealing with a commodity which can be packaged, stored and distributed to the consumer like other goods. It is not even tangible, although tangible products are often associated with it – souvenirs being an obvious example. The customer has to travel to the source of supply. Furthermore, the provision is more in the nature of a service which the Americans refer to as 'the recreation experience'. Active participation occurs at the source of supply – the site – although elements of the experience – particularly anticipation and reflection – occur back home.

The time and money over and above that required to provide for the basic necessities of everyday life is sometimes referred to as discretionary time and income. We are each, broadly speaking, free to do with them more or less as we fancy. The supposition that increases in discretionary time and income combine to guarantee growth in leisure pursuits may be encouraging for the leisure business in general but is not particularly helpful for specific enterprises hoping to benefit from such growth. It is one thing to say in a global sense that a demand or even a need for something exists, but unless a manager can gain access to the appropriate market and supply the something in question to the satisfaction of the customer, such general statements remain theoretical abstractions. Recreation is particularly susceptible to the difficulties of matching intangible wants with imprecise facilities.

People want experiences which are capable of stimulating a variety of pleasant sensations such as 'happiness'; 'excitement'; 'good humour'; 'well-being'. . . . These things cannot be supplied directly but can be stimulated by entertainment. Providing entertainment outside the home invariably involves land and buildings to a greater or lesser extent. Some forms of provision have lasting popularity while others are susceptible to, indeed often the product of, shifts in fashion or technology and are in a constant state of flux.

Buildings typically possess a high degree of permanence and inflexibility which make them susceptible to obsolescence – day-to-day use becomes poorly related to the original purpose of the facility. The more closely facilities are aimed at particular fashions, the more susceptible they are to the wasting effects of obsolescence. The performance of the facilities eventually declines to a point where redevelopment or refurbishment become unavoidable. If the level of use of recreational facilities is to be kept at its planned level as economically as possible, there is a constant requirement for the manager to monitor and evaluate changes and shifts in demand carefully. This does not mean, however, responding slavishly to every whim and fancy of public taste. If a proper balance between action and prudence is to be achieved, the analysis of demand – market research – which this requires must be undertaken in a systematic manner. Effective market research requires clarity of purpose if it is to have a firm foundation.

'Leisure' and 'recreation' are terms with little practical meaning without specific products or consumers in mind. The concept of leisure rests on an uneasy foundation of few facts and many general assumptions which are difficult to separate. Defining leisure and recreation is rather like defining good health – easier to define by reference to what it is not (in the case of health, by defining poor health). It can be difficult to define the precise nature of leisure activities and pastimes by reference to the benefits they bestow, for there may be wide variation in the perception of such benefits by each beneficiary. For this reason much of the analysis of demand is focused on the use or consumption of the 'hardware', sometimes in the form of land or buildings but more commonly the equipment associated with participation in particular pursuits.

4.2 CONVENTIONAL ECONOMIC APPROACHES TO DEMAND ANALYSIS

The first people really to get to grips with the demand for recreation were two American economists called Marion Clawson and Jack Knetsch (1966). They defined the recreation experience as having five interrelated facets, namely:

1. the anticipation and planning of the trip;
2. the journey to the site;
3. the time at the site;
4. the return journey;
5. the recollection of the visit.

They attempted to estimate the total benefit of the recreation experience and the price of deriving that benefit by analyzing these five features. In the case of enterprises not charging an admission price, the price was expressed in terms of the cost of undertaking the journey. They derived a demand curve for such sites by plotting the cost of trips against number of trips. Although this and other techniques of demand analysis which place heavy emphasis on the travel behaviour of potential visitors may be capable of some adaptation to reflect the true cost of travel (incorporating, for example, estimates of the value of travel time, ease of journey, etc.), recreation participation is essentially a matter of individual rather than aggregate behaviour. Furthermore, the commodity is not homogeneous in nature. It is heavily dependent on the visitor's own perception of the attractiveness of one site in relation to other substitute facilities. Clawson and Knetsch point out themselves that if one knew all the relationships involved and had reasonably accurate data for the magnitude of each factor in a given situation, one could estimate the volume of recreation that would be demanded, or how many visits a site would receive.

This American influence coincided, more or less, with the introduction of the Countryside Act, 1968 which, among other things, established the Countryside Commission for England and Wales. (Separate legislation applied to Scotland, establishing the Countryside Commission for Scotland.) These developments stimulated a surge of research interest in the U.K., mainly in the fields of economics and geography. A strong spatial theme ran through this early research, with particularly heavy emphasis on trip generation models. Dower's reference to 'The Fourth Wave' (1965) provided an evangelical rallying call to this 1960s movement. A more recent analysis of this topic is provided in *The Economics of Leisure and Recreation* by R.W. Vickerman (1975) or, better still *Sport and Recreation: An Economic Analysis* by Grattan and Taylor (1985).

The essentially spatial emphasis of research into the demand for or participation in recreation gave way to greater concern for the characteristics of participants. Roberts, for example, pointed out that in relation to recreational pursuits, what people actually do is probably less important than with whom they do it (Roberts, 1978). This fresh emphasis on the characteristics and behaviour of participants provided an insight into demand of more immediate relevance to site managers, although much of the sociological analysis of recreational demand did little more than confirm material propounded elsewhere in the behavioural sciences (particularly consumer behaviour in the USA) and applied more broadly to the determinants of consumer demand.

Economists seem to favour analysis of aggregated patterns of consumption, relying heavily on theoretical models to explain how such patterns are created and influenced. The British Tourist Authority survey of 1967 referred to in Chapter 1 highlights the inadequacy of the concept of aggregate demand for the purposes of site management. The manager is obviously concerned with patterns of consumption but made up of individual transactions with individual customers linked together (or so the manager hopes) by one or more common threads. Although this may only amount to two sides of the same coin, the perspective of the economist appears to differ from that of the manager with regard to patterns of consumption (or consumer behaviour as the manager may prefer to think of it). The emphasis which the social psychologist and sociologist places on the behaviour of groups – being partly the result of the modified behaviour of the individuals which comprise them, partly by the links which bind them together – is closer to the perspective which the manager of a market orientated enterprise must adopt.

4.3 BEHAVIOURAL APPROACHES TO DEMAND ANALYSIS

Much of this broader work had been explored in the 1930s and 1940s. In particular, A.H. Maslow studied the driving force behind individual behaviour, namely motivation (Maslow, 1943). His analysis identified the main components of this complex phenomenon and then ranked them in order of significance. In 1943 he postulated a hierarchy of five primary needs which may be summarized as follows:

1. physiological needs (e.g. hunger, thirst, warmth);
2. safety needs (physical security and protection);
3. love needs (affection, friendship and emotional security);
4. need for self-esteem (dignity, self-respect);
5. the need for self-fulfilment (success and achievement).

Adam Smith made similar observations almost 200 years earlier; however, although Maslow's classification has given rise to much discussion and interpretation, it still retains its significance as a working hypothesis.

When people's physiological needs are satisfied and they are no longer fearful about their physical welfare, social needs become important motivators of behaviour. These are such needs as those for belonging, for association, for acceptance by one's fellows, for giving and re-ceiving friendship and love . . . Above the social needs, in the sense that they do not usually become motivators until lower needs are reasonably satisfied, are the needs of the greatest significance to management and to individuals themselves. They are the egoistic needs and they are of two kinds.

1. Those that relate to one's self esteem; needs for self respect and confidence; for autonomy; for achievement; for competence; for knowledge.
2. Those that relate to one's reputation; needs for status; for recogni-tion; for the deserved respect of one's fellows.

Unlike the lower needs, these are rarely satisfied; people seek indefinitely for more satisfaction of these needs once they have become important . . . Finally – a capstone on the hierarchy – there are the needs for realising one's own potentialities, for continued self development, for being creative in the broadest sense of that term (McGregor, 1960).

The primary difficulty faced by managers in coming to terms with these concepts is that they represent continuous states of flux for each individual. The life-cycle alone, from cradle to grave, precipitates a continuous series of changes which affect motivation.

Each (individual) is influenced from birth by a succession of different forces, operating through different phases of the life-cycle. These influences are:
- personal (i.e. involve internal motivations as influenced by earlier experiences);
- interpersonal (i.e. stem from close relationships with other sig-nificant people, for example, family members, friends, teachers, neighbours);
- institutional (such as school ethos and curriculum); socio-cultural (i.e. the larger set of norms and values diffusely present in the culture).

These influences bind people together in a variety of social groupings and networks. (Rappoport and Rappoport, 1981).

Attitudes, values and motivations take on a rather different perspective when individuals are seen as members of social groups. The collective beliefs and attitudes of groups influence the economic decisions made by individuals. Patterns of individual behaviour are affected by the cultural and social norms which surround the individual, indeed a person's social existence can be characterized by their identification with groups. Group membership may be explicit in the sense that individuals sharing similarity of ideas or patterns of behaviour may display ostensible group identity, for example, family groups or clubs. Alternatively, behaviour may be implicitly characteristic of other individuals, in which case it may be perceived as being characteristic of a group; this is commonly associated with many recreation activities, for example, riding or motor cycling. People may shift from one social group to another as they participate in a succession of activities. Their role may differ from one group to another, revealing or reflecting different facets of their personality.

Depending on an individual's dominance within a group (displaying, for example, an ability to lead action or opinion) that person is subject to pressure from the group to conform to its values and norms. Usually, people become members of a group because they share its values and beliefs. Conforming to the principle of cognitive consonance, their attitudes tend to be reinforced by communication within the group. Sociologists use social stratification for distinguishing between and evaluating social groupings which tend to be given or expect different treatment, have different rights, duties and privileges, and hold views of the world and of themselves which are related to such differences. There are many criteria which could be adopted for this purpose. The most universally applied are social class, age, gender and, most commonly, occupation because this has been shown to be highly related to most other factors related to social class, particularly income and education.

4.4 CONSUMER BEHAVIOUR

Marketing requires knowledge of existing or potential consumers and understanding of individual behaviour. Obtaining information of adequate quality and quantity can be expensive while analysis and interpretation present numerous technical difficulties. The effort invested in market evaluation must, therefore, be carefully monitored to ensure that it is worthwhile. With this in mind, considerable research has been undertaken into the sequence of events leading up to purchase decisions. Building on the presumption that consumer behaviour is not random but based on routines which guide a consumer's decisions, models have been constructed to replicate the predictable elements of the 'purchase' process (Kassarjiam and Robertson, 1981). An illustration of such a model is shown below (Figure 4.1). The process starts at the comprehension level. This will be determined by the response of the consumer to the existence of the product and selling pressures associated with it. Numerous factors affect the search process and the selection and interpretation of information available to consumers. The interaction of these factors will encourage or inhibit the consumption process.

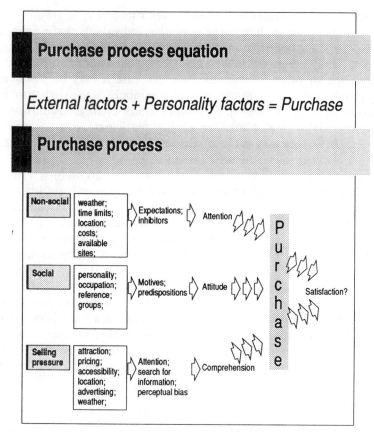

Fig. 4.1 A model of consumer behaviour for recreation participation.

The decision to expend time and money on recreation has three components:

● a set of motives;
● a choice of substitute courses of action;
● criteria, according to which the motives are matched with the choices.

In this context, motives (reflecting the needs underlying behaviour) are related to preferences toward a particular type of recreational pursuit, for example, informal countryside recreation; active sport; spectator sport; entertainment, etc. The choice of sites boils down to the sites and facilities which, according to the perceptions of the recreation-seeker, offer the potential for satisfying his or her motives – the 'evoked set' of choices. Purchase criteria are the rules which the customer employs to match his motives to the means available to satisfy them.

The 'evoked set' may represent only some of the opportunities of which the recreation seeker is aware and a still smaller fraction of the total number of enterprises technically available. Opportunities which a potential visitor may view as substitutes may not correspond to the same 'product class' which the provider attributes to the expected range of visitors. For example, the potential visitor may consider a scenic drive through the countryside to be an alternative to visiting a country house, whereas the country house manager may consider a visit to another house or historic building to be the most likely alternative substitute. Visitors themselves may hold quite different ideas of substitute facilities. This implies that the buyer's motives do have some order and structure against which purchases are evaluated. It also assumes that purchase criteria develop as the buyer learns about the environment in which the purchase occurs and the experience which consumption brings.

In the case of new, untried expenditure such as a visit to a new enterprise, buyers may only have an incomplete set of purchase criteria. This can be developed by learning from direct experience, the experience of others or information from a reliable or attractive source. Repeated satisfactory purchases may encourage the establishment of a routine behaviour in which purchase decisions become simplified and predictable. Such behaviour implies that purchase criteria are well established and that the buyer has strong preferences. The more buyers simplify purchase decisions, the less likely they are to seek information concerning similar purchases. Paradoxically, after a routine has been established, dissatisfaction may arise because of boredom or curiosity – all known alternatives may become unacceptable and new ones considered, deliberately complicating the decision process. Routine becomes re-established in the swing back to simplification.

4.5 MARKET-LED MANAGEMENT

The manager of a recreation enterprise must strike a balance between attracting those visitors who always seek something new and those who return even though this may be infrequent. The former may visit an enterprise once only or return only if there is something inherently new to enjoy. Few enterprises can rely solely or even heavily on a continuous stream of new visitors. Those uniquely popular tourist attractions, such as the Tower of London or Stonehenge, which appear to do so are usually internationally renowned or involve a strong element of pilgrimage such as Shakespeare's birthplace or the Blarney Stone. The phenomenon of 'brand loyalty' plays an important part, therefore, in the success of many commercial recreation enterprises.

Although research undertaken by NOP (National Opinion Polls) on behalf of the Countryside Commission for England and Wales has indicated that over half the population make at least one trip to the countryside per month during the summer, site loyalty (expressed in terems of sequential repeat visits) is low. Far from displaying the kind of homogeneity associated with grocery products or consumer goods, each site may be perceived as a unique 'product'; sites are not equally available and are seldom visited consecutively time after time.

The factors which stimulate visitor interest in a particular site arise from the properties of the site itself or some representation of it (such as publicity material). Invariably, the nature of the recreation experience being offered to the public is so lacking in homogeneity that it is difficult to explain simply. However, there are five broad headings under which the attractiveness of a site may be categorized:

- distinctiveness;
- quality;
- availability;
- quality of management;
- price.

The distinctiveness and quality of a recreational facility may be portrayed by the inherent attractiveness of a site (this may consist of physical attractiveness; historical attraction; participatory or entertainment value) and the comprehensiveness of the ancillary features which invariably enhance the primary attraction of the site. Availability is synonymous with the proximity and accessibility of the site and, within the site itself, the number of people which the site can accommodate without a significant deterioration in the enjoyment which they derive from the site.

What the manager requires is an indication of the relative influence of these factors in attracting or deterring visitors. This will vary from visitor to visitor according to the perception of each. While visitor reaction to those factors may be stimulated (with positive or negative effect) relatively quickly by raising or lowering visitor expectations, underlying attitudes toward them are likely to change more slowly, related to experience gained from other, comparable visits. It is important in surveying visitor reaction to these purchase factors, to establish as clearly as possible the visitor's frame of reference for the responses, in particular, to the other places which the visitor treats as comparables (the evoked set). A simple framework for undertaking such analysis is suggested in Figure 4.2.

Respondents should rank or score each of the purchase factors for each of the sites which is comparable with the site in question. Each respondent will provide a relative perception of the purchase factors. This will be a personal judgement but at least this method gives the manager some indication of what each judgement represents. If a recreational enterprise is not seen as a single entity but a collection of independent facilities related to, if not wholly dependent on, the overall enterprise, a similar analysis could be used to estimate the relative pressure to visit each facility.

Purchase Matrix

Purchase factor	Consumer perception			Weighting (subject site)
	site a	site b	site c	
Inherent attraction				
Quality of facitlities				
Variety of facilities				
Pricing				
Capacity of facilities				
Advertising				
Accessibility and signing				
Location and setting				
Weather				

Fig. 4.2 Purchase matrix.

Without the advantage of existing visitors to provide direct market research information, the next best source is that relating to more general patterns of recreational behaviour. For example:

- clubs and other organizations (sports federations, associations, national governing or co-ordinating bodies, etc.) responsible for the organization, co-ordination or control of recreation participation on a broad geo-graphical basis;
- bodies concerned with countryside heritage and conservation who have membership schemes (e.g. the National Trust) or who have house publications (e.g. English Heritage);
- national surveys of recreation participation such as the national recreation survey undertaken by National Opinion Polls on behalf of the Countryside Commission;
- regional surveys of recreation participation occasionally commissioned by such bodies as the Sports Council or regional tourist boards;
- local demographic information often held by local authority planning departments.

Figures derived from such sources may provide some basis for estimates of the broad parameters of the possible market for a new development. They may be useful in highlighting trends in recreation participation which may be less discernible from site-based information.

Marketing managers talk of the 'marketing mix', by which they mean the variables which can be used to influence consumer behaviour. These are commonly characterised as the four Ps, namely, product price, promotion and place. The term 'product' in this context, usually refers to the variety and quality of the product which is or could be made available. Price is largely self explanatory though it refers primarily to pricing structure and includes discounts, optional purchase prices (such as additional charges for special features). Promotion refers to advertising and publicity. Place refers to the accessibility of the site and its availability, therefore, to a worthwhile number of visitors.

A simple example may help in summarizing some of the practical considerations of demand analysis.

Nonesuch Park which consists of 40 acres of landscaped parkland surrounding a lake of 10 acres is adorned by a Georgian mansion with stables and assorted summer houses, gazebos and follies. The contents of the house are not of great intrinsic value but they do chart an interesting history of the family which owns the property. The house and grounds have been open to the public on occasion and these open days have proved so popular that the family decided to extend the opening onto a commercial basis if this could be justified and, so, a more accurate assessment of probable demand is now required.

Step 1

Check any existing primary data (i.e. relating directly to Nonesuch Park):

- previous visitor surveys;
- unstructured comments, e.g. visitors book;
- traffic counts.

Much if not all of this data will only be of anecdotal value because it was not collected for the present purpose, nor, possibly for any specific purpose. It is always possible to find more information but time and money invariably impose limits on this. Consider, therefore, whether or not obtaining further primary data is going to be cost-effective and can be collected in the time available.

If more data is to be collected, then the manner and timing of its collection must be planned.

Step 2

Set up a search for secondary data (i.e. data indirectly related to the subject in question) such as:

- demographic information for the geographic catchment area of the Park (obtainable, principally, from the district and county authorities surrounding Nonesuch);
- information regarding traffic flows in the area surrounding Nonesuch Park (obtainable from the highways departments of the district and county authority);
- information relating to other sites which, for one reason or another, are comparable with Nonesuch Park (possibly available directly from sites, if the managers are prepared to be co-operative; possibly from local tourist organizations – particularly the local regional tourist board);
- information about the local economy (these days often available from the closest business school or university economics department).

Step 3

Identify gaps in background information.
Estimate the importance of these gaps (to what extent will future decisions, particularly investment decisions, be affected by not having this information?).
Estimate the cost of obtaining the information.
Either obtain the information with the greatest precision and the lowest cost; *or* do without the information. In this case it is prudent to plan for the contingencies which might be appropriate, depending on the results of the information gathering exercise.

Step 4

Identify the operational objectives based on market expectations, for example:

- who will be visiting?
- where will they come from?
- who will make the decision to visit?
- who will be spending the money when they arrive?
- what will they expect to be able to do?
- how long will they expect to stay? How long does the site operator expect them to stay?

Objectives should be capable of expression in sufficiently precise form to be used as performance criteria.

Step 5

Prepare a feasibility report/business plan.

REFERENCES AND FURTHER READING

Clawson, M. and Knetsch, J. L. (1966) *Economics of Outdoor Recreation*; Johns Hopkins Press, Baltimore and London.

Dower, M. J. (1965) *The Challenge of Leisure*; Civic Trust, London.

Grattan, C. and Taylor, P. (1985) *Sport and Recreation: An Economic Analysis*, E & FN Spon, London.

Kassarjian, H. H. and Robertson, T. S. (1981) *Perspectives in Consumer Behaviour*, Scott, Foresman and Co., Illinois.

Maslow, A. H. (1943) A Theory of Human Motivation. *Psychological Review*, **50**, 370–96.

Maslow, A. H. (1954) *Motivation and Personality*, Harper and Row, New York.

McGregor, D. (1960) *The Human Side of Enterprise*, McGraw Hill, London.

Rappoport, R. and Rappoport, R. N. (1975) *Leisure and the Family Life Cycle*, Routledge and Kegan Paul, London.

Roberts, K. (1978) *Contemporary Society and the Growth of Leisure*, Longman, London.

Tourism and Recreation Research Unit (1983) *Recreation Site Survey Manual: Methods and techniques for conducting visitor surveys*, E & FN Spon, London.

Vickerman, R. W. (1975) *The Economics of Leisure and Recreation*, Macmillan Press, London.

Resource evaluation | 5

One of the essential aims of management is to maintain and enhance wherever possible the value of the resources involved in the production of the goods or services involved. Management performance can be measured in various ways, ultimately, however, management achievement must be measured against the value of the resources employed. The process of evaluation consists primarily of measurement and comparison. In many realms of management the resources employed are homogeneous (similar in form and nature). Measurements can readily be expressed in the universal medium of exchange (and comparison), money. Land and buildings are seldom homogeneous, they are heterogeneous. Indeed, in the case of recreational land management, more often than not, the more heterogeneous the better. In some cases, this means that a particular site can be so distinct, even idiosyncratic, that the value associated with it is so ambiguous that the valuer bases the value on the next best use which can clearly be identified and evaluated: thus introducing the concept of opportunity cost.

The subjective assessment of value is invariably based on data of limited validity, processed according to rules of thumb which may be useful in a pragmatic sense but can lead to severe and systematic errors. Three of the more common heuristic 'rules' are:

1. that something is typical or representative of a class, type or group and may be assessed accordingly;
2. that the likelihood of an event occurring may be assessed according to the ease with which examples can be brought to mind;
3. that people make estimates by starting from an initial value which is adjusted to yield the final answer.

However, these judgements may be insensitive to prior probability of results; sample size; misconceptions of chance and predictability. Furthermore, adjustments are often insufficent to provide proper comparability.

5.1 THE ROLE OF LAND IN THE PRODUCTION FUNCTION

In most businesses, costs which show little variation within the normal range of production seldom enter into day-to-day management decisions. The problems of day-to-day management tend, understandably, to focus on those costs which are expected to vary from day to day. It is normally assumed that a thriving enterprise should be able to cope with the cost of 'fixed' ingredients such as land, buildings and regular labour as a matter of course. Resource evaluation tends to be concerned, therefore, with the measurement and comparison of the costs of ingredients which vary on a day-to-day basis. The danger of placing too much emphasis on optimizing the ratio of daily (variable) costs to daily production is that when profit margins start to deteriorate the effect of 'fixed' costs can be devastating. Enterprises which rely on a high proportion of fixed assets, such as land and buildings, will quickly become vulnerable to a reduction in the volume of business because the cost of fixed assets cannot easily be reduced in line with reduced demand. The market value of an enterprise, even a non-profit enterprise, will be based primarily on the value of its fixed assets. A reduction in the value of business will be translated into a reduction in the value of the resources being employed. Ultimately, the point will be reached at which resources can be better deployed in some other use. Land and buildings usually represent a fixed cost of production, normally expressed as a rent or rent equivalent (e.g. cost of borrowing) which, in the short term, may relate only loosely to the type or volume of business which they accommodate.

In the case of urban recreation the difference or uniqueness of one site compared with another may be superficial; artificially created to enhance the appeal of the enterprise. The one factor which is universally accepted as being significant is location. In fact, the accommodation requirements (buildings) associated with urban recreation facilities tend to be stereotyped and will be treated as the primary capital asset of the enterprise. Indeed, enterprises funded by financial institutions are deliberately designed to be suitable for non-recreational uses such as industrial warehousing. In these circumstances, evaluation consists, crudely, of the following stages.

- Estimation of the gross rental value of the property, usually by comparison with similar properties, must take account of the location, form, condition, accessibility and flexibility of the building and, in the case of rental accommodation, the terms of the tenancy agreement. It must also take account of the profit capable of being derived from the operation and divided between the entrepreneur and the landlord.
- Deduction of the outgoings on the building associated with maintenance and repairs, property management and insurance will leave a net rental value.

● Capitalization of the net rental value by a rate of interest determined by the market's assessment of the risk associated with the investment.

This approach is inadequate for recreation enterprises which utilize land or buildings of great intrinsic value or which are unique to the extent that comparable current market data is unobtainable. Still, the notion of market worth acts as a powerful criterion against which enterprise performance will be measured in the absence of comparable market information.

The next most preferred method of obtaining a balance sheet value is to base the value of the enterprise on its revenue earning capability. From the gross turnover of the enterprise the costs of operation are deducted except for those attributable to:

1. a rental value for the land and buildings;
2. the investment income attributable to the capital invested in the enterprise, other than land and buildings (this may simply be the loan charges on the capital);
3. the management income sought by the operator of the enterprise for his or her entrepreneurial flair.

The latter two are sometimes lumped together as 'management and investment income'. The net profit figure is than allocated between a rent charge for the land and buildings and the management and investment income. In the absence of better information the split is normally 50:50. The rental figure so derived is then capitalized in the manner described above. Nevertheless, in many cases it is very difficult to arrive at a reliable value figure for the site and the buildings on it. In these circumstances, a more qualitative approach must be adopted. Qualitative approaches lack the conventionalized acceptability of financially based evaluation. They must, therefore, be as objective and systematic as circumstances permit.

The site requirements for most recreational uses in the countryside may or may not be capable of being stereotyped or even capable of expression in an explicit form. Recreational land managers rarely have the chance of selecting a site which conforms closely to an ideal specification even if it could be produced. More often than not, a manager will either be committed to a predetermined site (which may not be used for recreational purposes but possesses some potential for recreation) or be called upon to respond to an 'opportunity' to develop recreational uses on a site which has, possibly unexpectedly, come available. In these cases the scope for responding quickly or radically to demand is circumscribed by the constraints of the site and its location.

5.2 LOCATION FACTORS

The relationship between the location of a site and its accessibility to the people for whom it is intended to be attractive is fundamental to any

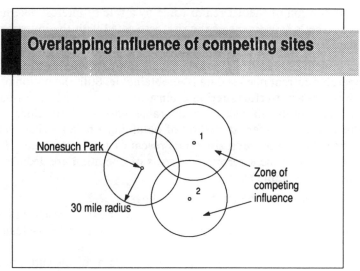

Fig. 5.1 Overlapping influence of competing sites.

evaluation. A 30-mile radius has often been cited as a rule of thumb measure of the distance that day-trippers will casually venture from home, by car. Rigid adherence to such general yardsticks can, however, be misleading and there may be substantial variation in the catchment area of different sites. The location of a site as perceived by a potential visitor may differ considerably from its true location, for example the journey may be short in distance but the route may be complicated or congested. Casual trippers may be diverted by competing facilities along the route. It requires, therefore, a degree of motivation or single-mindedness in favour of a particular attraction at a more distant location if a tripper is to persevere beyond more local, substitute destinations. In contrast, a site which can accommodate some facility or service which is complementary to a dominant recreational attraction may benefit from the draw of the dominant attraction. So the recreation manager must understand the scale and nature of the competition (Figure 5.1).

Attempts have been made over many years to evaluate location factors and to measure site accessibility for recreation projects. Early approaches to these issues involved the application of 'trip generation models' and 'distance decay functions'. However, these attempts to formulate accurate, reliable estimates of accessibility which would justify general application, proved largely fruitless in improving on the rules of thumb already mentioned.

Although managers are likely to have an intuitive working knowledge of the accessibility of sites under their control, they also need a proper appreciation of visitor perceptions of a site's accessibility. This can only be obtained from market research – in this case, information about their journey to the site, probably derived by questioning the visitors themselves along the following lines.

- Where did you set out from?
- Was it a spur of the moment decision?
- How did you find the way here?
- Did you think it was easy to find?
- Did you consider going elsewhere? If so, where?

It is important to distinguish between questions which seek factual information – where did you set out from? – and those which require a judgement of some sort – 'did you think it was easy to find?' In the latter it is important to understand how the judgement is guided; for example, it is necessary to have some details of comparable journeys which the respondent would class as difficult or easy.

The degree to which location preferences may be exercised is limited in the case of land uses which are low in the hierarchy of values. As a general rule, recreational uses are low on the list. In other words, there are competing land uses capable of sustaining a greater value for appropriate sites than a recreational enterprise could sustain for the same site. The greater the reliance of an enterprise on consumer attraction (particularly retail and leisure facilities) the greater the importance of consumer accessibility to the site. The number of substitute locations is inversely proportional to the degree to which consumer accessibility becomes critical. In the case of sites for countryside recreation, remote from town-based centres of demand, poor accessibility may be counterbalanced by the uniqueness or attractiveness of the site or counteracted by the marketing skill of the site operator or both. If, however, the success of a site is primarily the result of marketing skill, the value of the business lies in the management rather than the site. As the extent to which the unique properties of a site become important in its evaluation, the influence of subjectivity must be carefully monitored. This point, that management and marketing skills can affect the attractiveness of a site to potential customers, emphasizes that only some sites possess inherent attraction and that evaluation of demand can be an extremely imprecise art.

5.3 SITE ATTRACTION

Though accessibility and location make an essential contribution to the uniqueness of any piece of land, they are seldom wholly responsible for its value. The most positive influence on the value of a site in recreational use is its capability to attract visitors. If this is restricted by poor location, then the potential value of the site will not be realized. If a site has an outstandingly good location and the planning permission to develop it, then its ability to attract people can be artificially stimulated. It is preferable, however, for the power to attract visitors to be inherent in the site itself. This may occur for the following reasons:

- the site may be particularly well suited to an identifiable activity such as rock climbing or water sports;
- it may possess great beauty created by nature or man;
- it may possess natural curiosity or uniqueness – Land's End or John O'Groats, for example;
- some historic event may be associated with it, for example, a battlefield;
- it may possess particular scarcity, such as open space in a built-up area.

Natural or historic features of a site, including historic associations attaching to the site which might be exploited (see Chapter 10), should not be underestimated. Equally, their value should not be exaggerated if the benefits owe more to skilful marketing than characteristics of the site itself.

Assessing the attractiveness of a site for recreation is a two-stage process of identification (of the attractive features) and evaluation. The identification process is normally structured around a schedule or inventory, itemizing all the essential characteristics of the site. This is similar to the system employed in describing agricultural property. The purpose of a schedule of farmland is to identify and describe the distinctive elements of the farm which could contribute to its productive potential. In the case of a recreation enterprise the corresponding purpose is to identify the distinct elements of the site which could contribute to its overall ability to attract visitors and to accommodate them on site. This will, of course, be coloured by the operational objectives which have been established for the enterprise.

Evaluation relies more heavily on the assessment of relative virtues than absolute criteria. Undoubtedly, however, the difficulty of quantifying the qualities of a unique or unusually varied site is compounded by the lack of appropriate units of comparison. Recreational potential is sometimes considered almost synonymous with the capacity of a site to accommodate specific activities, subject to an appropriate level of capital investment. Matching the physical characteristics of the site with specific activities is a routine stage in site evaluation. The resource requirements for most recreation enterprises can be fairly readily expressed, at least in broad terms; indeed, there are standards of provision associated with many recreational activities, usually related to the population within the catchment area of the site. There will always be innovators, of course, pursuing new ideas, but seldom without some knowledge of conventional ways of meeting management objectives.

5.4 CARRYING CAPACITY

Recreation is about people so, whatever activities a site is capable of supporting, one objective will be to attract visitors. The manager must have an appreciation, therefore, of the capacity of the site to accommodate visitors. The day-to-day capacity of a site must take account not only of the number of visitors on site at any one time, but also the length of time they spend there. Half the number of people staying for twice the length of time is not the same as twice the number of people staying for half the time. Inevitably the transition from the range of possible activities to the final selection involves the application of management judgement.

The primary purpose of site evaluation is, therefore, to assess the capacity of a site to accommodate one or more recreational uses. This will entail identifying the attributes of the site capable of contributing to its use for recreational purposes and, equally, areas of particular sensitivity, vulnerability or physical restriction which limit the effective carrying capacity of the site. If a site is to be developed for recreational use, a balance must be struck between the ability of the site to accommodate sufficient visitors to make the development worthwhile, yet not so many that the use causes unacceptable deterioration of the site. Although, as a general rule, the larger the available budget the more visitors a site can be designed to accommodate, the law of diminishing marginal returns implies that there will be a financial constraint on any development. However, this is seldom the point at issue in the case of countryside recreation; the capacity of a site to receive, hold and release visitors is invariably determined by physical factors. Even though a site may be large in area, there may be pressure points which cause crowding and erosion, in other words physical deterioration of the site. This could also impair visitor enjoyment of the visit and reduce the likelihood of return visits.

There may be a tendency to resort to purely descriptive analysis to build a 'picture' of overall resource potential. The limitations of a pragmatic approach of this nature can, nevertheless, be reduced by adopting a systematic way of presenting the descriptive analysis in a tabular or matrix form, incorporating a scoring system for each resource component, such as a three or five point scale. Figure 5.2 illustrates a simple scoring matrix which could be developed using imperfect but practical information. Undoubtedly, there are many specialists in the various facets of resource evaluation, ranging from the ecologist to the landscape architect. Taking advantage of this expertise can be of great benefit, but the advice is likely to have its price and its cost-effectiveness should always be considered.

The potential contribution of individual activities may be judged according to the following criteria.

● Inherent attraction – the capacity of the activity to attract people without coercion (i.e. information as distinct from advertising hyperbole).

Evaluation matrix

Site factors \ Score	3	2	1	0	minus 1	minus 2	minus 3
area							
topography							
climate							
vegetation							
landscape quality							
open water (area)							
rivers and streams							
physical features (e.g caves)							
location							
accessibility							

Fig. 5.2 Evaluation matrix.

- The ability to hold the interest of visitors or, more particularly, to extend the time they spend on the site.
- Participatory attraction – the capacity of the activity to involve people in its consumption over and above mere passive involvement.
- Uniqueness – the sensitivity of attendance to the availability of substitute facilities.
- Sensitivity to statutory consents (which may reflect environmental values).
- Dependence on other resources, notably labour and capital.

Some facilities are considered to be ancillary but none the less essential to the efficient operation of primary activities (namely the main attractions). Some are of a service character and, typically, include catering and gift sales, but may be as mundane as toilet facilities. Others, for example, amusements and interpretation facilities, enhance the recreational experience inspired by the primary attraction. If a site is capable of supporting more than one activity, the manager must recognize that while a combination of some activities may improve the utilization of the site, some activities can be mutually exclusive, for example, using a lake for swimming, fishing and boating may be difficult without careful scheduling or physical zoning.

5.5 JUDGEMENT OF NON-FINANCIAL VALUES

So far, attention has focused on two of the essential components of evaluation, namely:

1. identification and description of the characteristics of the site in question;
2. measurement of those characteristics.

There is a third, vital component implicit in any evaluation and that is the value system which governs the basis upon which resource allocation decisions will be made. Although the first and second require accuracy and precision, failure to take full account of the third can reduce much diligent and painstaking effort to irrelevance. The value system which dominates land management decisions is based on financial value. Resource allocation decisions which ignore this carry a reduced chance of being effective. It is a powerful, ubiquitous value system; relatively simple, crude even, based on the universal medium of exchange – money. It is well suited to decisions based on simple objectives, uncluttered by caveats and constraints. Maximization of profit or wealth in the short to medium term exemplifies the kind of ostensibly unequivocal objective best suited to the market value system. Even so, the owners as well as managers of enterprises run, ostensibly, according to commercial objectives can underestimate the sometimes mercurial nature of financial value.

There are many items which can be costed and set against gross revenue until the net balance is attributable to the residual influences of land and managerial enterprise. In businesses where the standards and norms of acceptable performance are well understood, the annual value of the site will account for a substantial share of the profits. In enterprises where such standards are less clearly defined, the greater share of the profits will be claimed by the manager-entrepreneur while the share attributable to the site will be correspondingly less.

Market pressures move land inexorably and, from an environmental point of view, sometimes destructively to its most profitable use. The property market, the mechanism which stimulates this transition, is notoriously imperfect: it lacks uniformity and cohesion; it operates on the basis of unreliable, misleading information and, because of the permanence of the buildings with which it is developed, the time taken for it to correct its own mistakes is so long that the new effect is possibly as destructive as productive. The statutory mechanisms for controlling and overriding environmentally destructive effects are negative, inadequate and open to abuse. The mechanism for correcting mistakes is, to all intents and purposes, non-existent. These factors also have the indirect effect of generating a degree of scepticism toward new proposals for development which sometimes borders on paranoia.

Only in the case of rural land do natural attractiveness and ecological variety assume anything more than superficial significance in site evaluation. In urban areas a site should be in or moved (by market forces) to its most beneficial use. It should also be in the best location for that use and occupied by an operator with a proven record of success and reliability. These factors can all be reflected in financial terms. The process of valuing urban property is sometimes depicted as taking a 'snapshot' of the income flow which the property promises to yield at the time, converting this to a capital value by simple mathematical calculation. This static approach may be adequate for those involved simply in buying and selling property; however, estate management is not about dealing with a static scene, but with a continual state of flux. In the case of recreational land management there may, to use a theatrical analogy, be two productions competing for the same stage, each set in a different value system: the popular attraction features commercial management and performances are judged according to financial criteria; the 'serious' attraction features cultural values and attempts to resolve the paradox of balancing public access against the risk of damage which accompanies this.

The external benefits of amenity and recreation to surrounding areas, largely ignored by the market place, should be accounted for. Failure to do so permits the insensitivity of the market in allocating scarce resources to go unchallenged. If the challenge is to be mounted effectively, external benefits should, wherever possible, be expressed as financial benefits – the unequivocal language of the market. It is always simpler to communicate on any topic in a common language. In the case of land use, failure to use the language of the market place requires decision makers to adopt different value systems, so planners and their political masters (our elected representatives) can and must take account of the social, ecological and environmental values which the market fails to recognize. This runs the risk, of course, of idiosyncratic political decisions if the evaluation lacks rigour and objectivity (see Grattan and Taylor, 1985).

5.6 ENVIRONMENTAL IMPACT ASSESSMENT

Too often, recreation resource development follows a route which allows business people who will gain most directly from the development persuade local officials or representatives (some of whom may have business connections that would gain from the development) to support the development. The development is then vigorously pursued. Few questions are asked about a variety of costly social and environmental consequences. This only serves to confuse the true merits of the development. Such costly side effects can be minimized with adequate planning. It is important to identify, in advance, all the stakeholding groups affected by the development, how they will be affected, and how to plan to minimize the adverse consequences of the development to the stakeholders. It may not be immediately obvious precisely who the stakeholders really are. For example, plans to develop the recreational potential of a fishing river will clearly affect local hotels, restaurants and shops selling sports tackle. Less obviously, farmers, shoppers, and other recreation participants who are mostly members of the local community, will also be affected. There will also be effects on the natural environment of the river. Larger recreational projects may impose additional burdens on local facilities such as police, refuse collection, water and sewage provision, the costs of which will be passed on to the local community. Equally, important spin-off benefits may be generated such as local employment – an economic multiplier effect from visitor expenditure.

It can be difficult to identify and evaluate the true impact of any development, all the more so when the development itself occurs in a sensitive environment. The problem raises many complexities which have, in the past been dealt with in a relatively *ad hoc* manner. Now, however, regulations brought into force in 1988 in response to a European Community directive, require development proposals falling within certain limits to be accompanied by an Environmental Impact Assessment (EIA). The wording of the regulations gives rise to wide interpretation. However, in the countryside this will apply, typically, to mineral extraction or waste disposal schemes. However, each case is looked at on its merits and recreational proposals could easily warrant an EIA.

REFERENCES AND FURTHER READING

Beer, A. R. (1990) *Environmental Planning for Site Development*, E & FN Spon, London.
Grattan, C. and Taylor, P. (1985) *Sport and Recreation: An Economic Analysis*, E & FN Spon, London.
Ross, M. (1991) *Planning and the Heritage*, E & FN Spon, London.
Savoy, A. (1988) *Holistic Resource Management*, Island Press, California.
Tait, J. *et al.* (1988) *Practical Conservation: Site assessment and management planning*, The Open University, Milton Keynes.

<table>
<tr><td>**6**</td><td># Management planning</td></tr>
</table>

Management planning describes the sequence of decisions associated with allocating resources to achieve predetermined objectives. 'Planning' has always been accepted as one of the cornerstones of management; the others suggested by Henri Fayol (1959), one of the founding fathers of business management, being: organization, co-ordination and control. Although the purpose of planning is ostensibly self evident, the process and its application remain enigmatic. Each of the other three functions has a more definite purpose – to organize . . . something; to co-ordinate . . . something; to control . . . something. We plan *for* something – some future event, future circumstances – above all to meet the uncertainties which the future holds. Most people have an aversion to uncertainty: it carries with it the prospect of chaos, rejection and isolation. There is a preference, therefore, for dealing with things which are inherently more 'knowable' than forecasting and investing in the future. This may explain, in part, why so little has been written about this pro-active branch of management.

A management plan should provide a well structured and cohesive framework of decisions for the deployment of the resources available in a manner which maintains and enhances their value. There are distinct yet related classes of decisions which may be subject to incompatible influences. Igor Ansoff (1987) refers to three classes, namely:

- strategic decisions;
- administrative decisions;
- operational decisions.

Strategic decisions reflect the operational values which drive and direct the enterprise. They determine the relations of an organization with its external management environment (see also Chapter 3); they establish the criteria which will be used to judge the type of markets which the enterprise will set out to capture, the type and intensity of development and the effectiveness of the eventual implementation of the plan. Administrative decisions are concerned with the way in which the enterprise organizes its own resources; in particular, the organization and development of the staff and the organization and procurement of its capital resources (land, buildings, equipment, stocks, etc). Operational decisions are concerned with the budgeting and control of the operation of the enterprise. Many administrative and operational decisions will concern predictable reactions to predictable sets of circumstances. They will establish the nature and timing of predetermined responses. Such decisions are best thought of as policy decisions and should be clearly denoted in a policy statement.

It is impossible to manage an organization which lacks clear objectives, or more correctly, it is impossible to assess the performance of the 'management' applied to it. Every enterprise requires an explicit set of objectives which serves as a focus to guide the direction and range of the decision process. The management plan should weave together all the relevant decision areas to enable the objectives to be achieved as effectively and efficiently as possible. It is, in other words, an explicit and systematic prescription for co-ordinating all decisions which contribute to the enterprise achieving its objectives as effectively and efficiently as possible. Clearly, therefore, the more simple and unambiguous the objective(s), the clearer the focus of the management plan can be. Multiple or ambiguous objectives usually carry different values which will eventually give rise to value judgements which may be mutually incompatible.

6.1 STRATEGIC PLANNING

A balance must be maintained between strategic and operating decisions. If demand is expanding in a steady and predictable manner, technology is stable and customer preferences changing only gradually, attention is likely to be focused on the operating activities of an enterprise. Leaving competitive strategies to evolve slowly and incrementally is unlikely to undermine the success of the enterprise. In these circumstances, the evolution of the enterprise is a 'grass roots' process. However, even in such stable conditions some entrepreneurs may operate in a manner which is strategically aggressive, expanding the enterprise beyond the limits consistent with a stable, benign equilibrium. They may be compelled, as a consequence, to adopt aggressive operational management to sustain any success which the enterprise may achieve. For one reason or another, conditions will become turbulent and changeable. Strategy will have to be reviewed in order to maintain a proper relationship to external conditions. At this point enterprise managers can no longer afford to continue to be preoccupied with operations at the expense of strategy. Continued success, even survival, requires priority to be given to strategic activity.

However, the preparation and review of management plans demands time, concentration and patience. It requires more deliberate thought than managers customarily associate with the stereotyped image of the job of a busy, dynamic manager. Once complete, the plan should be a blueprint for future operations. Then the danger is that the blueprint becomes fixed; managers become reluctant to modify or review the plan even though they are in a position to use other information than that employed in the original plan. In other words, they fall into the trap against which Napoleon is said to have warned his generals, of 'forming a picture' from which they would not deviate, irrespective of its lack of resemblance to reality – the blueprint becomes a straightjacket. This, of course, becomes the justification for not planning for those who mistake management flexibility for chaos. Coping with chaos requires a different kind of plan.

Recreation is an excellent example of a type of service provision which lends itself to marketing management (as distinct from production management). The primary purpose of a recreation enterprise is to provide enjoyment and entertainment without prejudice to the safety and well-being of the participants, the natural environment and community at large. Provision of recreation facilities is the result of striking an acceptable balance between a market – an identifiable group of potential customers – and the resources available for development, in particular, a site with appropriate development potential. The footloose entrepreneur, unwedded to a fixed location, has greater freedom to adopt a more overtly market orientated approach than a landowner. A landowner is inevitably restricted in the selection of a site and by its attendant development constraints. In these circumstances one must make the best of what one has even if this may be little more than an area of land with no other beneficial use. The task of enterprise selection in such circumstances is not a matter of having a popular or fashionable idea in search of a suitable location, it is a matter of assembling, on a predetermined site, an enterprise, probably composed of a variety of commercial ingredients, which is commercially viable and which is unlikely to become obsolescent.

In complex developments the most attractive options are likely to be explored as sets of enterprise combinations. These will be examined and tested to assess how the components might function in operation, how well they might withstand the stresses and strains to which they could be subjected and which components may be particularly susceptible to crisis or failure. Decisions concerning the scale of the operation and its general *modus operandi* determine the impact which the enterprise will have on its environment. They will also determine the capacity of the enterprise to withstand unexpected changes in its environment. This whole area of decision making is concerned with connecting the operation of the enterprise to the environment. These main connecting strands will appear in the management plan as strategy decisions.

The term 'strategy' is conventionally applied to the art or science of warfare – this being one of the main antecedents of industrial management. However, in the modern context of management it has shed its specifically military connotation. It denotes a rule or set of rules for making operational decisions. This is sometimes confused with the term 'policy' which denotes a specific response to predictable, repetitive circumstances.

> A contingent event is recognised, such as a periodic need to work over-time, or a snowstorm. What needs to be done and the outcome of such contingencies are well known; the contingencies are repetitive, but the time of specific occurrences cannot be specified in advance. In view of this it is not worthwhile to require a new decision on what should be done each time overtime is needed or each time it snows. A better and more economical procedure is to prescribe, in advance, the response to be made whenever a specified contingency occurs. This is done through a written statement of the appropriate policy and of accompanying procedures for its implementation. Since the management decision is thus made in advance of the event, a rule for behaviour can be imposed on lower levels of supervision. Thus economies of management are realised, and consistency of action is ensured. (Ansoff, 1987)

It is evident, however, that policy in this context of a programmed response is a control mechanism. Strategy, on the other hand, is a directing mechanism.

The management objectives of an organization should be as simple as possible. If management is thought of as a path of achievement, objectives identify the point at which the path crosses the horizon into uncharted territory. If there are several points there will be confusion about how to deal with ambiguous priorities; to achieve all points simultaneously; to achieve all points sequentially (if so in which order) and so on. Even if the target is simple the path will be influenced by the starting point (bringing to mind the countryman's rejoinder to the lost traveller seeking his way 'well if I were you, I wouldn't be starting from here!') and the view of the number and scale of the obstacles which lie ahead. The strategy establishes the broad expectations of the route to be followed and the pace of progress. This will involve establishing operational objectives which have the dual purpose of waymarking the route and acting as checkpoints. It will also involve establishing policy themes which are likely to include:

- quality control (of the site and the service);
- visitor control;
- pricing and financial control;
- marketing.

6.2 MANAGING FOR QUALITY

The essence of quality control is that the product should meet or exceed the expectations of the customer. This is no place for a minimalist approach.

This kind of quality control should be ostentatious but not vulgar or over-intrusive. For example, a site must be kept clean and well maintained and must be seen to be so. In this respect Disney World in Florida serves as the standard which others try to emulate. Every piece of litter is meticulously cleared away, by hand, by an unobtrusive army of attendants, each uniformed in white. All physical components of the site stimulate visitor expectations of one form or another. Therefore, all facilities and equipment must be maintained in good working order; if anything is not in proper working order it should be substituted or withdrawn from service, with appropriate explanation. The standard of visitor service should also meet or exceed the expectations of the visitor. All visitors to the site are there for enjoyment – for some this will be synonymous with relaxation, for others excitement or activity – but coping with unfamiliar surroundings seldom contributes to immediate enjoyment (even if it eventually produces a sense of achievement!). There is no substitute for courteous, attentive staff to help visitors make the most of their visit. Clearly staff cannot be everywhere all the time, yet, there is great potential for visitor dissatisfaction with their perception of the service available to them. Every opportunity should be taken to reduce this potential by informing and reassuring visitors.

6.3 SITE PLANNING AND DESIGN

Visitors should be received into any site as smoothly as possible and should be encouraged to to distribute themselves around the site in a way which makes best use of the carrying capacity of the site. The movement and dis-tribution of the visitors should be in the nature of a flow – movement should be steady, uniform and, above all, predictable. This requires a degree of 'work study' to ensure that the design of the individual elements and layout of the site are appropriate to the enterprise. In cases, such as house opening operations, which are centred on existing buildings, 'work study' should highlight places where overcrowding might occur. Over-crowding produces frustration and anger among visitors which will detract from their own enjoyment and reduces their responsiveness to all but the most blatant visitor control.

Equally, the site must be designed to be more than a human 'sausage machine': visitors must be able to enjoy, at their leisure, the full range of facilities on offer. This also requires careful attention to layout, siting and design. Maintaining a social environment in which visitors appear to have great freedom to enjoy themselves requires a surprisingly large degree of visitor control. That environment has to be created and cultivated but in a manner which is as unobtrusive as possible. A standard of behaviour to which all visitors to the site would be willing to conform has to be estab-lished. In other words, the standards of the worst behaved visitor should not be permitted to mar the enjoyment of others. However, such control should be exercised in a manner which is sufficiently unobtrusive to avoid any feeling of discipline or coercion. This requires more than sensitive management, it requires a psychological awareness that is incorporated into the design of the site:

- the use of boundaries and barriers – to enclose, to exclude, to encourage, to screen;
- the use of coloured and textured surfaces to encourage or discourage the flow or distribution of visitors;
- discouraging pinch-points and bottlenecks unless they serve some purpose (such as pay points and even they should be as painless as possible).

6.4 FINANCIAL PLANNING AND INVESTMENT

All enterprises must have regard to the financial performance which they are expected to achieve. Broadly speaking, this may be considered as the relationship between expenditure and income over the planned life of the enterprise. No enterprise exists without expenditure of some form or other, invariably expressed in financial terms, and is usually expected to yield a flow of benefits which may or may not be expressed in financial terms. Expenditure occurs in the form of fixed capital, working capital and in the form of running costs. Most financial plans are based on the expected annual flow of income and expenditure.

Items of capital expenditure – fixed capital incurred in the initial development and consisting mainly of land, buildings and plant and machinery; and working capital mainly attributable to the cost of stock required to keep the enterprise running – are converted to an annual equivalent sum. This may be the annual cost of borrowing plus repayment of the capital in question; it may be the amount which the investor could have obtained as an annual income by investing the capital in the next best acceptable investment. Such annual payments normally start immediately the capital is taken up, irrespective of whether the enterprise is operating or not. Care should be taken, therefore, to phase the development of any enterprise so that premature dependence on development capital is avoided. The financial plan should indicate the quantity and timing of development (fixed) capital.

The pattern of expenditure on the day-to-day running of the enterprise varies. Some running costs remain at a relatively constant level irrespective of the level of activity, for example expenditure on regular, permanent labour. Some costs vary more or less in proportion to the level of activity, for example expenditure on casual, seasonal labour. Some costs are relatively infrequent, for example, expenditure on advertising. Generally speaking, costs which remain relatively constant are referred to as fixed costs and those which vary according to levels of activity are referred to as variable costs.

Most large scale enterprises carry a large proportion of fixed costs (including the annual equivalent costs of capital). Because most recreation enterprises are also seasonal in nature, expenditure is incurred each year before any revenue is received. As the season builds up, the income flow should quickly overtake the accumulated variable costs and start to recoup the accumulated fixed costs and eventually produce a surplus for survival to the next season. This pattern is known as the cash flow and for most recreation enterprises is a critical area of management performance.

6.5 PRICING

Although, these days, the general public is accustomed to paying for recreation, charges for entry or car parking are, nevertheless, a deterrent to most visitors. Most would prefer to pay less than the asking price. In the absence of detailed knowledge of what to expect of their visit, visitors adopt a lower expectation than implied by the entrance price to minimize the risk of their own disappointment. This initial apparent mismatch is justifiable provided that when the visitors have completed their visit they believe they have received good value for money. This can, in part, be assessed by reference to the length of time which visitors pass in enjoyable recreation. There are other types of recreation which provide accessible, though imperfect comparisons, such as football matches or cinemas, the entrance prices of which are there for all to see and which relate to a specific time span. For countryside recreation, a few enterprises (generally the larger ventures) establish the 'top of the market' and the majority of the remainder fall into line according to how they compare with the competition (including National Trust properties).

There is little doubt that the Disney organization leads the international market. They, emulated by many others, employ a comprehensive admission price which includes all attractions. Only things which may be considered extras incur additional charges – typically gifts and refreshments. This type of pricing policy is designed to minimize the resistance generated by repeated demands for money; but visitors musts be given a clear indication of everything included in the comprehensive admission price to dispel any suggestion in the mind of the visitor that they are buying a pig-in-a-poke.

Price discounts are justifiable on two grounds. The less important of the two is established custom (e.g. reductions for children). The more important justification is that the discount should generate more income than it costs. For example, a conditional discount, such as a voucher for a reduced or zero admission price for the holder if accompanied by at least one other adult paying the full price, may attract visitors who would not otherwise have bothered to visit.

Paying customers are a most valuable source of market information. Information provided by them enables the manager to:

- check the relevance of assumptions made in forecasting potential demand and market catchment areas;
- assess the effectiveness of advertising expenditure;
- assess the extent to which visitors are using the visit as it was designed, e.g. how long they spend on site; how much money they spend;
- assess how the visitors judge their visit (i.e. how they decide whether or not the visit came up to their expectations and if not, the extent to which it fell short).

The latter point, in particular, requires some elaboration. It would be naïve to think that this information may be obtained by asking visitors the direct question. It is human nature to give coded answers to such questions. Without understanding the code, therefore, the answers mean little. However, the code is seldom elaborate and, in a nutshell, the manager needs to discover the visitor's framework of comparison. This can be achieved by asking the visitor to compare the enterprise in question with other sites which he or she believes to be comparable with the study site.

6.6 PROMOTION

People sometimes believe, mistakenly, that the terms 'marketing' and 'selling' are synonymous. It is more accurate to say that good marketing should make selling superfluous. Marketing (including market research) means identifying market needs; interpreting them as a product or service; presenting this to the market in a way, shape or form which the market expects or for which it is ready; informing the market that such a product or service exists and how it may be obtained. No further pressure or coercion (namely selling) should be required to dispose of the product.

Such a neat and efficient aim is seldom achieved. The reasons lie in every part of the marketing and distribution process susceptible to Murphy's Law that if something can go wrong it will do. Promotion is the effort required to overcome the imperfections of the market process. Unfortunately, it may be misused to overcome more fundamental deficiencies. For example, promotion may distort the true nature of an inappropriate product to coincide with market tastes. This type of promotion is often applied in an aggressive manner but, even so, its effectiveness is short-lived.

Some forms of recreation have a clearly defined and well understood identity. The decision to become a purchaser may be made by an individual for purely selfish reasons. Other forms of recreation have a complicated identity and the decision to become a purchaser may be made collectively. This applies particularly to recreational visits made as a family unit. In these circumstances, selling recreation is inhibited by public ignorance of the precise identity of the product and of its availability. This may, in part, be overcome by promotion and advertising. As a rule of thumb 10–20% of the financial turnover of the enterprise might be allocated to this.

6.7 ENTERPRISE SELECTION

Choosing enterprises to include in a development is essentially a sieving process. The net is cast as widely as possible to start with. Many activities and options will be dropped from further consideration for reasons already discussed which render them impractical or unacceptable in some way. Those which remain in the net have to be sorted into the most appropriate combination to meet the objectives of the enterprise. Appropriateness is judged largely in relation to the values which underlie the objectives of the enterprise and could be financial, physical, aesthetic, cultural or social.

There is a series of questions, outlined below, which must be asked in determining the choice of main venture around which an enterprise is to be developed. The first group of questions relates to demand and will determine the possible enterprises which might be contemplated.

- Is there a demand which can be attracted to and accommodated on this site?
- What is the expected market profile?
- How volatile is this demand likely to be?
- Does the enterprise possess sufficient commercial significance to meet the full costs of provision?

The answer to the first question will come from market research, the object of which is, essentially, to impute to each person who could conceivably visit the site a likelihood that they will do so. This is dealt with in more detail in Chapter 4. The second follows directly from the first. The manager or developer of a site anywhere other than in the busiest urban locations should not be trawling for simply anyone who happens to be passing with an hour to spare for a casual visit. The site and its facilities should be designed to take the best possible advantage of what it has to offer. This means having an eye for the types of people who will derive maximum benefit from visiting the site and, at least in the case of a commercial enterprise, are prepared to convert that benefit into willingness to pay for the visit. This profile should then be matched with the socioeconomic profile for the geographic catchment area.

The history of recreation provision provides a catalogue of fads and fashions which proved to be short-lived and quickly became as redundant as yesterday's news. Most sites, especially those in the countryside, need to develop the goodwill associated with an enjoyable visit. In this respect, fashionable enterprises should be viewed with great caution if they are expected to have more than short-term popularity. Few, if any, recreation enterprises make huge profits. Some, indeed, make no profit after all costs are properly accounted for and some are subsidized by the provider (usually unwittingly in the case of private sector provision but knowingly in the case of public sector provision). Development costs normally take several years to recoup. Even the crude economy of the fairground is based on a three year cycle: the first year to pay for the facility; the second to write it off; the third yielding profit. Some ambitious ideas for recreation developments have foundered because the development cash flow was so tight that the site had to be opened prematurely with disastrous commercial consequences – once the public votes with its feet, it is inordinately difficult to repair the damage.

In the field of competitive innovation, being first in the market only matters if you stand to lose by not being first. Answers to a subsequent group of questions will determine the place of the enterprise in the market – leader or follower.

● Does the enterprise accord with the expectations of the owner?
● How unique will the enterprise be?
● Can the enterprise benefit from others which are unique?

The first of these applies particularly to private owners. Often the owner will not know the answer to this question until too late and it may be necessary to explain the full impact of the enterprise before development is embarked upon. It is not uncommon to find examples of ostensibly successful enterprises which have been terminated prematurely from a commercial point of view because the owners found that the extent to which they had to sacrifice the quiet enjoyment of their property was unacceptable.

Some element of uniqueness, even if it is simply outstanding quality of provision, can be contrived on most sites at a cost. There is a danger, however, of confusing contrived uniqueness with superficial gimmickry. Genuine physical uniqueness is most valuable if it falls into the category of 'awesome'. Examples which spring to mind include: Land's End, Stonehenge and Blenheim Palace. Historical uniqueness is helpful, usually as a device for making a visit interesting; for example, Shakespeare's birthplace or the Tower of London. Sites which are not outstanding in their own right may benefit from the reflected popularity of those which are. Sites close to or inside National Parks often benefit from this advantage but probably the most widespread example in this country occurs in proximity to the seaside or other large bodies of water.

6.8 ANCILLARY ENTERPRISES

Clearly the selection of the main venture is a major preoccupation – it is likely to set a tone for the whole enterprise and to operate as its commercial anchor. However, in all but the simplest of enterprises the main venture will require ancillary services which may be profitable in their own right, may only break even or may run at a loss (though adding to the overall attraction of the main venture). Gift sales and catering are the two most common examples but another important example consists of what are termed 'amusements' (gaming machines, computer games, etc.). Although visitors would probably not bother to travel to the site specifically to play on those electronic games, nevertheless they will use them if they are available. Unfortunately, these machines are not designed to blend unobtrusively into the wholesome and otherwise relatively tranquil surroundings of a stately home or country park. They are not easy to integrate into a rural recreation enterprise and many operators have found that they are too obtrusive or disruptive to justify.

The role which ancillary ventures play in the enterprise as a whole varies. Enterprises which attract very large numbers of visitors (several million per year), can become so capital intensive that the profit element of the admissions income is largely offset by the cost of the capital investment. In such cases, sales of merchandise of one form or another may be central to the profitability of the enterprise. Enterprises which have established themselves on the strength of one main attraction – say a historic house or museum – may develop by broadening their market appeal. In these circumstances, features which may originally have been ancillary – possibly a minority diversion from the main feature such as an adventure playground to entertain children who may otherwise be bored looking round a stately home – may be developed into something more comprehensive which become important attractions in their own right. Special events may be classed as ancillary to the main feature but, if they are sufficiently spectacular, they may be valuable in advertising the main enterprise.

Innovation is not unique to any one sphere of activity; however, there are examples of good and bad practice in managing innovation. Having good ideas is a good start but successful innovation requires more than this. Incremental development provides a safer route to long-term success than a blockbuster of an idea. Many people admire the success of recreation enterprises such as the National Motor Museum at Beaulieu without realizing that its origins lay in a much smaller enterprise which proved so successful that a new museum complex eventually proved necessary. A similar story could be told for Alton Towers which was attracting hundreds of thousands of visitors a year in the 1930s – well before the current spectacular development there. As projects get larger more people become involved, and more communication and co-ordination time is needed. A commonly practised approach to innovative development still rests on the notion that somewhere there is a customer who will want the product of 'a good idea'. Most good ideas do not come from marketing departments, sales departments, competitors or top managers but from customers. A report by the management consultancy Arthur D. Little entitled *Technological Change* published in 1991 cites an example of a study into the European truck industry and the time it took nine competitors to develop a new vehicle. The best performer, a US manufacturer, spent two years in the planning stage and a further two years to complete the development project: the worst performer, a European company, spent eight months in planning but took more than six years to complete the development project.

Some managers clearly believe that management planning is something which happens only occasionally – maybe on a change of ownership – and once the plan has been prepared it is carefully stored in an inaccessible place, only to be produced on express request. Meanwhile, the day-to-day management proceeds largely unaffected by the plan. This, of course, is like preparing a route for a forthcoming journey and then embarking on the journey without further reference to the map. Those managers who delude themselves that management plans lack the flexibility to cope with the day to day crises which occur should give serious consideration to the degree of forward planning which goes into proper crisis management. Whatever they may think they are doing, it is only masquerading as management as a means of concealing their own managerial shortcomings.

REFERENCES

Ansoff, I. (1987) *Corporate Strategy*, Penguin, London.
Technological Change (1991) Arthur D. Little Consultants, London.
Fayol, H. (1959) *General and Industrial Management*, Pitman, London.

<table>
<tr><td>

7

</td><td>

Site monitoring
and control

</td></tr>
</table>

It is common practice for enterprises of all types to submit for external scrutiny an account of the resources they utilize. Land and buildings are normally presented as assets. Indeed, the value of property may account for a substantial proportion of the 'book' value of an enterprise. Sometimes, however, managers consider land and buildings to be a liability: ostensibly, they make no direct contribution to the production of goods or services, yet give rise to fixed costs in the form of a rent charge, rates, repair and maintenance, insurance and management. At the other extreme, managers involved in the production of primary commodities, notably, agricultural produce, timber and minerals, consider land to be their primary asset. Land used for recreation seldom has a tangible product such as timber in the case of woodland: it gives rise to a service commodity. The features of the site manifestly contribute directly to the attraction and, therefore, to the continuing success of the venture. The site is in every respect an asset and must be managed accordingly.

7.1 COMMISSIONING THE ENTERPRISE

The gestation period for the design and commissioning of a recreation enterprise may be measured in years rather than months. Eventually, however, the operational objectives will have been set, the development plans brought to fruition, the designs implemented and the public admitted. Many of the basic premises upon which the development is based are little more than informed guesswork. The pre-development appraisal may have been systematic and objective but, nevertheless, susceptible to misconceptions of predictability, chance and representativeness. Forecasts or presumptions will have been made about the match between what the enterprise offers and the demand for that which is on offer. The effectiveness of the enterprise will, to a large degree, depend on the closeness of that match.

This is no simple matter and will involve a series of interrelated issues concerning the quality of the service provided, the reaction and behaviour of visitors on site and subsequently, as they decide whether or not to visit again or even recommend the visit to others. Most recreation resource managers would subscribe to the goal of providing a high quality recreation experience. However, this is a fuzzy objective which is difficult to define in operational terms. Its acceptability relies heavily on subjective perception to which, moreover, other people's perceptions are presumed to correspond. Unfortunately, substantial differences exist between managerial and user perceptions of locations, designs, facilities, supervision, maintenance and level of service to the visitor. A high quality recreation experience is one which meets or exceeds the expectations of each visitor. The resource manager exerts a critical influence, therefore, on the quality of the visitor's experience. Once an enterprise has been constructed it is commissioned or brought into operation – brought to life. It will then function in a dynamic environment; the visitors are seldom a constant factor, neither is the site nor the facilities on it. The essence of day-to-day management is that the enterprise should be made to function in the way it was designed to function and to provide information which will enable the original design to be revised and improved.

In response to the difficulty of measuring and monitoring visitor expectations which are capable of wide variation, resource managers developed surrogate measures intended to depict the essential constituents of the recreation experience. This led, in turn, to the development of performance standards. Standards have been developed and used by public agencies and private recreation enterprises to achieve quality control from initial design to day-to-day management. Although they have been developed for what sometimes appears to be every conceivable aspect of the recreation experience, they relate primarily to standards of provision, use and management. One area, central to the management of recreation enterprises, where there is a conspicuous lack of standards is staff selection and training. As a general rule, far too little time and attention is paid to this vital component of quality of service.

Setting standards is one thing, meeting them is another matter. It is imperative that a constant link be maintained between the design 'blueprint' and the actual operation. This will not be achieved without deliberate effort, for it may be more convenient for the site manager to put the original blueprint to one side and allow the enterprise to 'plough its own furrow'. This link between planned and actual operation is maintained by the control function of management. It will not exist unless deliberately addressed in the management plan and without deliberate effort on the part of the site manager and those to whom the manager is responsible. The two major components of control are perception and reaction. Perception requires knowing where to look, how often to look there and what to expect to perceive. If what is sensed deviates from expectations, then it is necessary to know what action, if any, to take. This is the reactive component of control. Being able to take the right kind and amount of remedial action at the correct time is essential to the control function. There may come a point, for example, when it is more cost effective to renew a facility (e.g. a building) than continuing to meet the cost of maintaining it to the appropriate standard. The ability to control depends on the ability to monitor or measure actual management performance, day by day and cumulatively, against the performance envisaged in the 'blueprint'. Measurement is a primary component of any control mechanism. This should indicate four principal things:

1. the effectiveness with which the day-to-day management meets the expectations esstablished in the 'blueprint';
2. the efficiency with which this is achieved;
3. the realism of the 'blueprint' in anticipating the performance of the enterprise, bearing in mind the characteristics of the site and independently derived standards of performance;
4. the extent to which the 'blueprint' needs to be modified to ensure future success.

7.2 THE POLICY STATEMENT

'Policy' can be viewed as the set of rules which defines the control function for an enterprise. These rules identify deferred decisions which will be triggered by the occurrence of specific circumstances. The management plan for the site should include a statement of policies which establishes a framework of standards. These standards should represent the norms and expectations which form the frame of reference to be applied when determining the extent to which the enterprise is on course to meet the operational objectives established for it. The policy statement should identify key components which are likely to influence the overall performance of the enterprise and should establish the criteria against which performance will be measured. The policy statement should identify:

● key components of the management plan;
● how they are to be monitored;
● the mechanism for communicating that information to a control system;
● the parameters within which control action should be triggered;
● the action which should be taken.

The controller intercepts, translates and responds to information collected and transmitted by the monitor. The monitoring system should reflect the factors which determine enterprise performance. For example, the site manager may wish to monitor the extent to which:

- the facilities are used by the people for whom they were intended;
- the facilities are used in the manner intended;
- the fabric of the enterprise is presented and maintained in an acceptable manner;
- the capacity of the enterprise is adequate;
- the capacity of each physical component of the enterprise is adequate;
- the level of service provided to the visitors is commensurate with the quality of the enterprise, i.e. the quality of the experience is commensurate with that which is expected (or paid for).

The manager will also need to monitor the effectiveness and efficiency of the enterprise, including:

- the level of harmony between different visitor groups;
- comfort of visitors and staff;
- the deployment of resources;
- legal requirements – contractual, tortious, statutory;
- environmental impact.

When performance falls below par, corrective action should be taken: this is the function of the control mechanism. It may be likened to the conditioned reflex in animals; it is a predetermined response to particular circumstances. Two questions arise:

- when should a response be made?
- what form should it take?

Corrective action should be taken according to the set of rules contained in the policy statement. This may appear rather pedestrian but although the measurements required may appear simple, most measurements also require a qualitative judgement:

- what is 'adequate'?
- what is 'presentable'?
- what is 'quality' and how could it be improved?

Establishing the action to be taken when performance deviates from standards becomes a strategy choice dictated by policy. However, the liberal exercise of managerial judgement is not in accord with the notion of policy. Authority should be exercised in support of policy to encourage implementation. The use of judgement should be reserved for circumstances in which satisfactory policy cannot be developed.

7.3 VISITOR FLOW PATTERNS

Most recreation enterprises involve engineering a flow of visitors to achieve the best use of the facilities which are available. Sometimes this involves encouraging an effective distribution of the visitors over the site or through the buildings. Sometimes the flow will be designed to follow a definite, often sequential pattern. This may start with a presumption that a significant number of visitors will arrive in a vehicle which must be parked in a convenient fashion. Once visitors have been parted from their vehicle, it may be necessary for access or admission to the site to be organized in a systematic manner, possibly because they need to be informed about the site; possibly because they are required to follow a prescribed route around the site (either for their own benefit or for that of the site); possibly because they are to be charged for admission.

Visitors may have expended considerable effort and expense in getting to the site, frequent returns may be unlikely and the enterprise may represent experiences which are new or infrequent. For these reasons, the manager should ensure that once visitors are admitted into a recreation enterprise they experience as much as is available to them as possible. If visitors are required to pay for admission, by the end of their visit they should perceive that the experience was worthwhile in relation to the expenditure. In an effort to achieve the best use of the site on the part of visitors, many enterprises encourage some sort of flow pattern around the site. In some respects this might be thought of as a 'critical path' in the sense that there is likely to be a pattern and volume of flow which represents the 'best' way to experience the site. 'Best' may, of course, be viewed either from the perspective of the visitor or the enterprise; ideally both perspectives should be congruent.

The critical path will normally consist of a series of nodes joined in series or in parallel by connecting routes. The nodes are points at which visitors are expected to pause and congregate in their journey through the enterprise. They should coincide with the primary attractions of the site, secondary attractions or ancillary facilities such as shops or restaurants. Nodes and connecting routes must have sufficient capacity to accommodate the flow of visitors. It may be uneconomic, particularly in relation to the main attractions, to provide sufficient capacity to accommodate fully the number of visitors present at times of peak demand. This will result in congestion capable of producing undesirable consequences such as extra wear on the facilities or visitor frustration and disruption to the normal flow pattern. Such consequences will have a detrimental effect on the experience intended for the visitors and on the site itself. If left unchecked this will establish a destructive cycle of deterioration and enterprise failure. The more activity at the node departs from its planned pattern (its expected pattern from the visitor's perspective), the more difficult the task of maintaining an enjoyable visit at that point.

It is imperative to monitor the extent to which overall use of the facility corresponds to its planned pattern of use. Based on the presumption that the longer the time which visitors spend on site the greater their enjoyment, length of stay is the criterion most universally applied in this respect. In the case of an enterprise with wide market appeal it is necessary to monitor the length of stay of distinct market groups or segments. This is particularly so on sites which accommodate activities which are not mutually compatible. The greatest problems in this respect are encountered in water-based sports, angling and boating, for example, though other land-based conflicts such as walking and riding can be equally problematic.

Most visitors, even those who have been before, will be in unfamiliar surroundings, indeed for many of them their surroundings will be alien. They require guidance to obtain the best from their visit. Such guidance is a service to the visitor and, as such, should be incorporated into the design of the enterprise. Equally, however, the same guidance is an important element of visitor control. It enables the manager to distribute the visitors in a way which maximizes the carrying capacity of the site. There are essentially three ways of communicating information to visitors on site:

- direct, person-to-person communication;
- indirectly by visual and aural aids;
- indirectly by written word or symbolic notation.

The first normally involves a guide. It is synonymous with a high quality of service but also enables a very high degree of control to be exercised over visitor behaviour by direct policing. It also carries, of course, a high associated cost. The second normally involves the use of film or tape of one form or other. This can be a most effective way of conveying information about the enterprise to visitors but the level of control is lower. It is, however, a most effective aid for staff training and can, therefore, play an important indirect role in visitor control. The use of symbols or written word may be used as a primary means of conveying information but may also be used as a means of reinforcing information conveyed by means previously mentioned. Such information may be conveyed collectively by sign or individually by leaflet or more elaborate publication. The direct policing element is almost totally absent. However, the written word is often used to convey messages of warning or prohibition. In this role it is often used as a reinforcement for direct policing of the site.

7.4 QUALITY CRITERIA

It is important that the manager understands and monitors visitor perceptions of quality. These will be largely determined by the environment from which the visitor has come (source rather than destination), applied to the quality of the experience and are likely to focus on quality of:

- natural resources – scenery, vegetation, water, trails;
- primary facilities – artificially created attractions;
- ancillary facilities – lavatories, tables and other site furniture;
- signs of congestion and overcrowding – waiting, noise, litter, erosion, conflict, fear, embarrassment, danger, interpretation, information, enforcement of rules, level of service.

The manager must maintain the right balance between maximizing the value of a visit (as represented by the benefits enjoyed by the visitors) and minimizing the cost of providing the intended quality of recreational experience.

Where the primary management objective is to accommodate large crowds enjoying many types of outdoor recreational activities, extensive maintenance may be necessary to sustain this objective. This requires regular, periodic attention to keep the site, buildings and fixed equipment in good order. Too often when the cost of new landscape work, new building or fixed equipment is being estimated, little account is taken of maintenance costs. Over the years such 'costs in use' can amount to as much if not more than the original cost of the building. Wherever possible the need for routine maintenance should be designed out of any development. Initial investment which is minimized at the expense of costs in use could prove false economy.

In some forms of production the quality of the product is not judged by reference to the quality of the conditions under which manufacturing takes place. In these cases maintenance of buildings and plant is a low priority, almost totally ignored unless statutory requirements are being contravened. Conversely, being seen to maintain the highest standards of quality and safety are likely to be operational imperatives for a site used for recreational purposes. Regular maintenance is an almost inevitable feature of the day-to-day management of a recreational enterprise, e.g. removal of detritus of previous visitors and ensuring that the site is safe for public use at all times. These are tasks which require constant monitoring and immediate corrective action. The monitoring task can and should be undertaken by all staff providing routine visitor services. Indeed a commitment to both elements – quality and safety – should be part of the management ethos to which all staff must subscribe and which should demonstrate the operational values of the enterprise.

7.5 MAINTENANCE POLICY

Maintenance cannot necessarily be undertaken as soon as the need arises. It may require skilled staff, special equipment or may require components of the enterprise to be taken out of service until repairs can be effected. Such maintenance requires a maintenance plan rather like the service schedule on a motor car. There are certain things such as the physical condition of a building which must be kept under observation on a systematic basis. Some building components have a fairly predictable life span under given operating conditions, for example the life of light bulbs or painting, which may be changed on a planned, routine basis. Other components may only justify repair or replacement if they are faulty. They require routine inspection because if faults are found, the damage to which they may give rise may develop rapidly if not rectified, for example the condition of the main structural elements of buildings.

Nevertheless, an awareness of the 'stitch in time saves nine' concept in relation to the operating costs of land and buildings should be part of the management ethos of any recreation enterprise. It is common for employees to apply strict demarcation to their areas of responsibility. Those who see themselves as being primarily concerned with the delivery of recreational services often consider property running costs as 'someone else's problem', arguing that costs are outside their control for a variety of reasons. For example, energy consumption depends on the design, construction and maintenance of the building, its sytem of heating and lighting, etc.; cleaning hours are determined by the 'central management'. Attitudes such as these conflict with good management practice. Control of all costs and the maintenance of quality should both be regarded as important responsibilities of the enterprise operator as well as the owner.

How much should property cost to use? The total annual cost of land and buildings will include the capital costs of acquisition and development expressed on an annual basis as debt or rent charges, the cost of the administrative overhead and property outgoings. Outgoings might include:

- building maintenance;
- energy (heating, lighting, power);
- cleaning and caretaking (wages and materials);
- rate charges (the uniform business rate);
- grounds maintenance;
- insurance;
- depreciation on fixtures and fittings.

Precise costs and the relative proportions in the composition of total cost will vary according to things such as age, design, state of repair, location, etc. Low expenditure in one area is likely to be compensated by high costs in other areas. The Audit Commission handbook on local authority property management states that 'Excluding the capital costs of a property, analysis of a range of buildings over a large number of authorities shows that as much as 25% of the total cost of providing the service . . . may consist of property running costs'. The report also states that four categories of expenditure account for nearly 95% of property running costs; broken down they are as follows:

Maintenance	20%
Energy	23%
Cleaning and caretaking	29%
Rent and rates	22%

Clearly there will be wide variation in the property running costs of different recreation enterprises, for example, in the case of a country park the cost of grounds maintenance is likely to be proportionately higher than in the case of a leisure centre. Wherever possible, however, a building or area of open space should be considered as a cost centre. In cases where the enterprise is dominated by one building or area of open space, the running costs should be broken down into primary cost elements.

7.6 TRANSLATING RESULTS

Collecting basic cost information is one thing. To be fully effective, information such as this must be translated into a form which alerts the manager to the need for corrective action and must, therefore, be available at the appropriate time. This means that relevant information should be provided on a sufficiently regular basis, to enable the manager to react if action needs to be taken. Cost information which is published once a year in final accounts, well after the costs have been incurred, may be useful in setting budgets for the following year but useless in assisting the budget holder to monitor current expenditure. Cost information alone has limited use in exercising control: invariably it should be related to other information on, for example, building use, size, capacity, number of occupants and other characteristics. Simple performance indicators can then be constructed analysing, say, cleaning costs per square metre or per visitor. For most types of building there are three main 'units' which are relevant for comparison purposes:

- area;
- capacity;
- number of occupants.

The manager must maintain the correct balance between preserving the assets of the enterprise yet minimizing maintenance expenditure. In this as in most aspects of management the feature which highlights the distinction between defensive, reactive management and proactive, responsive management is a proper plan. This should establish a clear framework for maintaining control of the operation of the enterprise and the expenditure associated with it. It should address the need for planned maintenance which is predictable and routine, the need for future maintenance requirements and control of maintenance expenditure.

Financial monitoring and control

8

The purpose of management control is to correct implementation of the management plan so that it conforms to predetermined standards. This cannot be achieved, however, without first identifying and measuring actual performance and comparing the results with other standards. For this reason monitoring and control are often considered two halves of the same function. The object of monitoring is to identify and measure change. It is a continuous process which may be linked to a control system but is aimed, primarily, at forecasting and anticipating the eventual outcome of current events. For example, a tachograph in a lorry or coach monitors and records the essential signs of the progress of the vehicle. The records may be used for future decisions concerning the way in which the vehicle is employed; they may also be used to analyze particular events which occurred during the time to which the records apply. It is important to bear in mind, however, that statistics are not, in themselves, indicators of performance. They must be related to specifically stated objectives if they are to be useful in appraising performance.

The object of control is to highlight circumstances which, because they deviate from a predetermined norm, require some kind of attention or corrective action. In some circumstances corrective action may be triggered automatically. By itself the tachograph is only monitoring, not controlling but if, for example, it was decided that a vehicle should not exceed a particular road speed, a control mechanism could be linked to the tachograph to prevent the vehicle from exceeding the maximum speed. It is also worth pointing out that operating policies are invariably control mechanisms. It is a misconception to believe that the term 'policy' is synonymous with proactive management; it is more commonly a feature of reactive management, often used as a pretext for adhering to a particular management dictum.

Financial performance is a key indicator of performance for almost any management organization, irrespective of whether or not it has a commercial objective. Financial monitoring is concerned with identifying and measuring changes in income and expenditure over a given period of time seldom shorter than one day and seldom longer than one year. For most reporting purposes the period is relatively long – quarterly or yearly figures. Most organizations are obliged to report, at least once a year and often more frequently, to owners or shareholders or trustees or a committee as well as to the Inland Revenue and H.M. Customs and Excise.

Such reports usually record the magnitude of income and expenditure. Although they may show a true record, they may not provide the manager with the information which indicates the transactions which materially change the financial position or direction of the enterprise. The annual accounting cycle to which most enterprises conform does not necessarily correspond to the information cycles appropriate for decision making. Many decisions are ill-structured and subjectively determined. It is difficult, if not impossible, to control that which cannot be measured, but costs must first be identified before they can be measured.

Monitoring which is designed to inform the day-to-day management of the enterprise must be sufficiently responsive to enable corrective action to be taken if necessary. For most general management purposes, monitoring systems have to be robust, rapid in yielding the information required, and intelligible to a reasonably well informed observer. Measurements of income and expenditure alone are seldom in a form which is immediately intelligible to a manager. They need, therefore, to be presented in a form which requires the minimum of additional information. In most circumstances the income and expenditure flows are related to the class of physical objects to which they relate, for example, the area of a building or sales counter; numbers of visitors; stock items in the gift shop. In other words, measurements of income or expenditure often need to be expressed as ratios.

8.1 PERFORMANCE MEASUREMENT

Most forms of management are driven by the concept of performance. Management should not only be effective in achieving operational objectives, it should be efficient and economical in doing so. Management success comes from performing ahead of that zone described in so many school reports as 'could do better'. This, of course, begs the question 'better than what?' – 'better than a mean or median value; better than the next best; better because the person or organization concerned has shown that they are capable of better? Performance is something which must be capable of identification, measurement and comparison.

At a strategic level performance may be viewed as the overall relationship between what is achieved – the flow of benefits – and the expenditure or cost incurred. It is often thought that information indicating a flow of benefits is on the 'good news' side of the 'good news v bad news' equation while information indicating costs is, of course, on the 'bad news' side. This is an inappropriate way of thinking. The framework for implementing management action is constructed from patterns of expected value which should determine the yardsticks against which management performance is measured. Both costs and benefits should be related to expectations, actual costs to expected costs and actual benefits to expected benefits. Thus 'good news' is represented by management performance relating to either benefits or costs which are better than expected. It still begs the question 'was this performance the result of a windfall gain or the result of deliberate management action?'

Effective management will achieve net benefit rather than net cost. Benefits in particular may be measured in several ways including social welfare or ecological benefits; a net benefit may even occur when net cost is lower than the expected amount. Benefits are usually perceived and measured as a value which is not always easy to express in simple financial terms. On the other hand, costs are invariably measured in financial terms. The discipline of cost control appears relatively simple compared with analysing the real value of the benefits produced. Furthermore, the difficulties in defining and measuring values often contribute to misplaced justification for prevarication over cost control.

Few management organizations pay equal regard to the measurement and control of both benefits and costs. In very broad terms, the thinking behind organizations which believe that the key to their survival lies in paying greater regard to maintaining a flow of benefits rather than minimizing cost will be inclined toward marketing, leaving production to fall in behind. Those paying greater regard to cost control may be thought of as placing greater emphasis on production management than marketing. In the case of marketing management emphasis is placed on maximizing benefits while in the case of production management emphasis is placed on controlling costs.

Most enterprises whose 'product' is a service provided for a substantial number of customers, place greater emphasis on marketing than production. The smaller the number of customers – the more exclusive the service – the more the emphasis is likely to shift to production and quality control. Generally speaking, the provision of leisure and recreation is perceived as lying closer to the marketing end of the spectrum than the production end. This is not universally the case but reflects the importance of generating and maintaining an acceptable, though often fluctuating, flow of benefits. The benefit which enterprises most commonly receive is an income flow. The benefit which customers receive in the form of the recreation experience is less simple. It involves a mixture of elements comprising the whole experience. The relationship between the price of the experience, the cost of providing it and the customer perception of value for money is less clear cut than in the case of a tangible product or an essential service.

8.2 MANAGEMENT RATIOS

Ideally, managers should be provided with a single key ratio that indicates unequivocally the degree of their success – their overall effectiveness. Even if this is possible, the key ratio will often need to be supported by subsidiary ratios indicating how performance can be improved. These may change with circumstances; nevertheless, the number of subsidiary ratios should be kept to the minimum. Consequently, it is essential that they relate clearly to overall success and only to matters which the manager is in a position to act upon. The relevant costs and benefits required for decision making are those which will be affected by the decision. The ratio of the cost of obtaining information to the likely benefit to be gained from it must always be borne in mind.

Most, if not all ratios must be related to and be capable of comparison with a standard to determine whether or not they indicate acceptable or unacceptable performance. Such standards may be established according to an organization's own past performance or according to budgets, targets or forecasts set by the organization itself. There is a limit to which internally derived standards retain credibility if set without reference to external standards such as corresponding performance figures for other similar organizations, especially 'benchmark' figures from organizations which are acknowledged as leaders in their field.

Many of the more common financial ratios compare income or expenditure with the assets employed in their generation. The main categories are as follows:

Fixed assets – used for the purpose of producing goods or services and which it is not intended to trade. This category would normally include land, buildings, plant and machinery.

Current assets – trading assets including stocks and debtors.

Operating assets – the sum of fixed and current assets.

Long term borrowed capital – debentures, preference shares and long-term loans such as mortgages.

Short term borrowed capital – overdrafts, trade creditors.

Equity capital – total assets minus borrowed capital and including ordinary shares.

Maintaining financial liquidity is of great importance in the case of recreation enterprises which are heavily dependent on cash flow. The ratios normally employed to measure liquidity are

$$\text{the current ratio} = \frac{\text{current assets}}{\text{current liabilities}}$$

$$\text{the 'quick' ratio} = \frac{\text{quick assets}}{\text{current liabilities}}$$

A current ratio of 2 or more used to be regarded as prudent in order to maintain creditworthiness, but in recent years a figure of about 1.5 has become quite normal. The 'quick' ratio excludes stocks because they may take time to convert into cash. A quick ratio of less than 1 indicates that the enterprise would be unable to settle up immediately with its creditors.

Priority ratios for the general manager or chief executive concern the relationship of the organization or enterprise with its markets; its providers of capital; its suppliers; its employees; its use of assets. How well the market likes a firm's products is normally gauged by the rate of growth of its sales. Most recreation enterprises have a finite capacity and their growth is restricted. This is one of the reasons why the value of recreation enterprises is based on the underlying value of the property rather than the value of the business itself. When recreation enterprises need capital it is usually raised by loans which are secured against the assets of the enterprise thus minimizing the exposure of the lender to risk. Provided the terms of loans in respect of repayments of interest and capital are met, providers of capital will be content with the financial information contained in the annual accounts of the business. However, the manager will need to monitor the effect of fluctuations in interest rates on the cash flow of the enterprise if capital is borrowed on variable rates of interest.

The performance of suppliers should be gauged according to price, delivery and quality. It may be uneconomic to monitor the price of all items used but a practical compromise would be to list purchases in descending order of value and measure changes in all items that account for (say) the top 80% by value. Dissatisfied employees will, if they can, vote with their feet. A chief executive should, therefore, monitor the turnover within the workforce and may also wish to monitor the average age of the workforce. Income per employee is also important. In the case of enterprises which are heavily dependent on fixed assets, the manager will be concerned about the ratio of actual output to maximum output, which will be governed by the capacity of those assets. If the organization is divided into divisions or departments, the general manager will want to monitor the performance of each. The operating profit of the department can be related to its operating assets according to the ratio of operating assets for each department to the total capital of the enterprise.

8.3 COST ANALYSIS

Ratios are not the only financial tool employed by managers. Where costs can be clearly allocated to clearly identifiable income-generating components of the enterprise, the terms 'cost centre' or 'income centre' are used. The magnitude and distribution of the costs and expenses associated with a revenue-earning enterprise are fundamental in determining its financial position. The analysis of enterprise costs has two primary functions: first, to provide yardsticks of performance between enterprises; and secondly, to estimate the extent to which costs affect performance (measured against the expectations raised by the objectives set for the enterprise). Many of the problems of cost accounting arise because data derived for one purpose are used, inappropriately, for another. Typical reasons for misallocation or non-allocation of costs are:

- expenditure not actually made is not recorded even though a cost item exists; for example, some house owners organize the opening themselves but, because they do not pay themselves, no expenses for 'management' are recorded;
- expenses which are relatively insignificant in relation to other estate enterprises may be 'lumped in' with larger sums;
- difficulty in allocating expenses which are not entirely attributable to the enterprise, particularly if the enterprise has little commercial significance;
- historic costs may not reflect the true cost of opportunities forgone in using assets to achieve a desired objective.

Capital expenditure normally results in the acquisition of an asset. It may be subdivided between fixed capital (e.g. buildings, plant and equipment, major fixtures) and working capital required to maintain a stock of consumable or short-life items. Operating or running costs are normally incurred in day-to-day expenditure. However, this is simply a widely accepted convention and not an absolute rule; the two are sometimes 'juggled' by stretching or varying the distinction between them. For example, if there are tax allowances on some items involved in construction (such as plant and machinery) but not on others, it may be acceptable in the interests of minimizing a potential tax liability to classify as many of the components of the construction as plant and machinery when, in other circumstances, this would be pedantic. Similarly, a pragmatic approach to the system of financial allocation sometimes results in apparently irrational allocations between the two heads (this applies to public sector accounting in particular). The gross cost of items of capital or revenue may be reduced by grant aid of one form or another. However, receiving grant aid may be conditional upon accepting obligations concerning future use, which may generate revenue costs.

It may be convenient to think of investments in buildings as once and for all payments, with a possibility of annual loan charges as the only continuing item of expenditure. Unfortunately things are not so simple. Once a building is put to use costs are incurred. These are referred to as 'costs in use' and describe the running costs of a building. Life cycle costs go even further and describe further items of capital expenditure which may be required to keep the building fully fit for the purpose for which it was designed.

For all but the very largest recreation enterprises, the main source of revenue is visitor admissions (or accommodation in the case of tourism). Admissions income is usually centred on the adult admission price but there are often discounts available for some categories of visitor such as children. Total admission income cannot, therefore, be calculated by simply multiplying the number of admissions by the adult admission price; the true income will almost certainly be less than this. It should also be remembered that because enterprises are seasonal in nature, costs will be incurred before the main season gets under way. In other words, the season is likely to start with a negative cash flow. The profitability for the year is influenced by the speed with which the cash flow becomes positive. Other sources of revenue will include:

● catering;
● gift sales;
● rides;
● special events.

Correspondingly, the main heads of variable costs will consist of:

● wages of temporary or seasonal staff;
● cost of stock sold (i.e. opening value of stock plus purchases less closing value of stock in store).

Conventionally, variable costs are those directly associated with a revenue centre which vary in proportion to the value of the volume of activity. Some enterprises may have additional variable costs.

In contrast to variable costs, fixed costs are conventionally considered to be those which do not vary materially with incremental changes in the volume of business. They will include such items as:

● salaries of permanent staff;
● advertising, publicity and public relations;
● rent;
● rates;
● energy costs;
● telephone;
● stationery and postage;
● consumables (cleaning materials, etc.).

If all costs are properly taken into account, many recreational ventures (probably over 50% of the total number) operate at a loss. Most ostensibly achieve a margin over variable costs but fail to meet all fixed costs and still leave a profit. To use the terminology of business management, most achieve a positive gross margin yet many are left with a negative net margin. Where a recreational enterprise is run almost entirely on the back of other enterprises such as a farm, this may not matter – the fixed costs may exist in any event as part of the primary function of the farm; the marginal cost attributable to the recreation enterprise may be insignificant. Even in the case of a freestanding enterprise a similar position may not matter for a short period of time but, in the absence of financial support – a grant or subsidy – from other sources, will quickly lead to insolvency.

The gross margin is commonly employed as a financial ratio providing a rough and ready indication of the performance of an enterprise either in relation to a primary factor of production – normally site area or per employee – or in relation to the main source of revenue – normally per visitor. It is widely used in farm management where the value of the main factor of production – land – is relatively stable and, for arable enterprises in particular, unit area is a good surrogate for value. In the case of livestock enterprises it is common to use the livestock unit as an additional measure. In the case of recreational enterprises, site values are unreliable. The market for recreational sites is fragmented and highly imperfect. Values are highly dependent on the value of the 'goodwill' associated with the enterprise and, therefore, closely related to the profitability of the enterprise. Sometimes, a key feature of a recreational enterprise will be a building or piece of land which has no value for any other use; it may, indeed, be a financial liability (often the case with historic houses). Only in the simplest of cases, therefore, will site area be a good surrogate for value. On a different scale, it is sometimes said that photographic film is the most profitable item sold in a gift shop in relation to the area of display and storage space which it occupies. This may be useful in considering the range of items to be stocked for sale but is only of peripheral interest in measuring the performance of the gift shop within the overall enterprise.

Broadly speaking, the financial discipline which competent land managers adopt in the financial control of agricultural enterprises should be equally, if not more rigorously, applied to recreational enterprises. Most can be divided into cost and revenue centres which can be separately monitored and controlled. It is important to remember, however, that they are probably not capable of independent survival – they rely on each other. Just because one cost centre looks to be less profitable than another is no reason for scrapping it but good reason for looking carefully into what is happening. (Otherwise gift shops would end up selling nothing but photographic film.)

8.4 COMMERCIAL THRESHOLDS

The main feature upon which a day-visitor venture is based usually involves admissions income. If the main purpose of the enterprise is to provide accommodation (including self-catering, camping, etc) the position will be slightly different. Nevertheless, the way in which profits are generated varies according to the size of the enterprise, which is often expressed by the number of visitors admitted during the course of the opening season. The largest ventures are, of course, international and attract millions of visitors each year. Probably the largest is Walt Disney World in Florida which admits in the region of 12 million visitors per year. In this country the nearest equivalent in a rural setting is Alton Towers with visitor admissions in the region of 2 million per year. Such large enterprises generate their own trading environment but are so rare that there is little merit in further discussion of them here.

At the other end of the spectrum, annual attendances in the range 10 000 – 20 000 are normally considered so small scale in commercial terms that they fall into the category of a hobby. This is not to say that they are badly run nor that those running them lack enthusiasm and dedication. It is simply that unless each visitor is paying a large admission price or the enterprise is subsidised in some way, such a small number of visitors is unlikely to generate sufficient income to cover the true costs of operation.

Somewhere in the middle of these extremes lies the more usual size of enterprise. At visitor levels in excess of 20 000 they can no longer be classed as hobby enterprises; staff will have to be employed and other costs of operation incurred. This region can spell danger for the fledgling enterprise trying to expand. There is a cost threshold although in the short term the income is inadequate to cover the costs of operation. Unless this threshold is overcome this size of business is doomed to fail – this is the commercial graveyard where many perish. As a general rule of thumb, the level of day-visitor attendance associated with a reasonable expectation of producing a true net surplus is 100 000 visitors per annum. There are, of course, enterprises which, at first sight at least, appear to confound the commercial graveyard rule of thumb. Even so they should be scrutinised very carefully to obtain a true picture of financial performance.

In the case of a reasonably successful commercial enterprise one might expect to discover the following financial profile:

- variable costs amounting to 80% of day visitor income;
- variable costs on catering and gift sales amounting to 20% of corresponding turnover;
- management costs in the region of 15–20% of total income;
- advertising costs in the region of 10% of total income.

It must be emphasized that these ratios are very broad indications of expected performance. Every enterprise is unique, however, and financial profiles will vary.

There is a wide variety of recreational enterprises which may be found in the countryside, particularly the urban fringe. The variety tends to increase rather than decrease with new ideas emerging all the time. Enterprises which were once features in their own right tend to become absorbed into the broad menu of provision. Nature trails are a case in point; once endemic in the countryside they are now one facet of the wider field of countryside interpretation rather than an end in themselves. Farm-based interpretation now includes study centres, farm open days and guided tours as well as self-guided trails. The direct financial return of such facilities may be unattractive, though the more that is offered the greater the scope for levying some kind of charge.

8.5 TAXATION

The impact of taxation on profits and the extent to which losses may be set off against other taxable income are important to individuals, partnerships or companies operating a recreational enterprise in the private sector. The rules regarding the taxation of income and capital are established by statute. The rules are, at times, complicated in expression and application and it is not intended in this short section to go into details of the law.

Most recreation enterprises with a commercial component are concerned first and foremost with the generation of income or the minimization of losses. Income tax is an annual tax levied on the annual income derived from an enterprise. Income is measured on the normal basis of the adjusted profits shown in the annual, audited accounts for the tax year beginning on 6 April. Income tax is charged under six schedules described by the letters A–F. Schedule A applies to income derived from land; Schedule B used to apply to woodlands income but is now out of the tax schedules; Schedule C applies to certain kinds of government interest and dividends; Schedule D is divided into a number of cases of which Cases I and VI have particular relevance; Schedule E applies to income from offices, employments and pensions and includes PAYE; Schedule F applies to income in the form of dividends from UK resident companies.

A Schedule D Case I assessment is applied to a trade (which often includes recreation and leisure). The taxable income is computed according to the profits of the taxpayer's accounting year ending in the preceding year of assessment. Not all expenses which are incurred in the course of trading are deductible. The Income and Corporation Taxes Act, 1988 (section 74) gives a list (qualified in some cases) of those which are not deductible but there is no corresponding list of those which are deductible. Generally, however, any expenditure, of a non-capital nature, incurred wholly and exclusively for the purpose of that trade, justified by commercial expediency and incurred for the purpose of enabling the trade to be carried on and be profitable is deductible. In certain circumstances expenditure on capital items can be reflected in the computation of annual profits by capital allowances.

Where profits are assessed under Case I, losses may be set off against future profits in the same trade or, for a limited period and only on election, be set off against the taxpayer's other income. Where the trade is run by a partnership, the partners are liable for tax on their share of the partnership profits. Where the trade is run by a company, Corporation tax and not Income tax is payable. In this case, while the profits will be computed on normal accounting principles, Corporation tax is charged on those profits as they arose in the financial year during which they were earned. A company's trading losses may be set off against future income arising from the same trade or against profits (of whatever description) of the accounting period in which the losses arose.

There are circumstances, for example historic houses open to the public on a limited basis, in which profits are not deemed to be earned in the process of a trade but are treated instead as casual profits arising under Case VI. Tax is then charged on the full amount of the profits arising in the year of assessment (i.e. on the current-year basis) and related, therefore, only to the surplus of the receipts over the expenses which were necessary to earn them. Furthermore, statute makes no mention of any allowance for deduction of expenses. When an enterprise is assessed as a trade under Case I, expenses are more generously allowed than when it is assessed under Case VI. Where losses are made under Case VI relief is available on them only in so far as they can be set off against other Case VI income accruing to the taxpayer in that or the subsequent year and no relief is available against the taxpayer's income from any other source.

The movement of capital assets from one ownership to another may give rise to a liability for tax either by virtue of the capital transferred and/or the capital gain if such a gain exists. Capital Gains tax was introduced in 1965 but, in broad terms, now applies to gains accruing since 31 March 1982. Because in times of high inflation an element of capital gain may be attributed to general inflationary trends, gains which have arisen since 1982 are indexed to strip out the effect of inflation. The basic event on which capital gains depends is the disposal of an asset. Inheritance tax (previously Capital Transfer tax) depends merely on the transfer of capital and could apply, for example, in the event of the death of the owner resulting in the transfer of ownership under the terms of the will of the deceased. It is beyond the scope of this book to consider the fiscal planning inherent in a disposal or transfer of the assets of the enterprise which may give rise to Capital Gains tax or Inheritance tax. This kind of tax planning is a subject in its own right.

<table>
<tr><td>9</td><td># Budgeting and measures of performance</td></tr>
</table>

9.1 PREPARATION AND USE OF BUDGETS

Before a final decision can be made about the establishment of any commercial venture and most not-for-profit ventures it is essential that budgets are prepared showing the predicted income and expenditure for the enterprise once it has been established. Every business takes time to settle down, to build up its markets, to regulate its expenditure, to judge its staffing levels, to tighten management control and to gain the willing co-operation of all those involved. Until this process has been completed the business will not be on an even keel. In the meantime, only the practice of actually running the business will show what, if any, modifications should be made. Before reality can have its full influence, the preparation of an initial budget must be to some extent a matter of guesswork. Advice will be sought from comparable ventures, but only as the business runs will it be possible to prepare budgets which are reliable indicators of future performance: even then predictions may turn out to be wrong. Because of inherent uncertainties initial budgets should not be too optimistic and must indicate clearly how they have been put together and the assumptions upon which they have been based.

There will be many possible combinations of forecasts, each producing a different result. However, a budget can only be a guide to action if the budget-maker decides on and sticks to one combination: otherwise the confusion of choice will confound ultimate decisions. The initial budget will show predicted income and expenditure after the business has settled down and may be accompanied by a statement indicating how long this position may take to achieve. It may be reasonable, in any given instance, to anticipate a loss in the first year or two. Such a loss will have to be made good and must be included in the cost of establishing the business over the first few years. It is advisable also to prepare a 'break-even' budget showing the minimum turnover necessary to prevent the business from making an actual loss. The definition of 'break-even' depends upon circumstances. In the case, say, of a new estate enterprise which is only one of many, a no profit/no loss definition may be enough; whereas in the case of a business on the proceeds of which the proprietor has to live from the beginning, break-even may have to be that level of profit which will provide the minimum income necessary to prevent the operator's personal bank account from exceeding its overdraft limit.

The initial budget will show the extent of the predicted income and the outgoings necessary to earn it. The net profit expected may be insufficient to achieve the financial objective. At that point, consideration will have to be given to the extent to which, if at all, the budget can be altered. Is the predicted income reasonable? Can any costs be less? Are staffing levels too high? Are the staff to be paid too much? Perhaps some items of expenditure could be pruned. Perhaps, on the other hand, the expected income is too great. Budgets need careful analysis before they can be wholeheartedly accepted; indeed part of their purpose is to set in train detailed enquiry.

To the extent that expenditure is under the direct control of the manager, it may be easier to forecast and control than income, which may be more susceptible to the uncertainties of the interaction between the goods and services to be offered and the prices set. One level of demand may be expected at one price and a lower one at a higher price (other things being equal). Which will produce the greater profit? There may be latent demand which, with efficient marketing, can be tapped. A demand may be created for new goods and services to be offered. Customers may be enticed from competitors. The price at which goods and services can be offered is, to a degree, controlled by the existing expectations in the market; but the quality of what is offered and the sector of the market in which the product is made available will also affect the price which could be asked. As already stated, the assumptions, predictions and information (volume and quality) upon which budgets are based vary; the purposes for which they are prepared also vary. Nevertheless, the manager must address the points raised above; points which have, indeed, been made in earlier chapters of this book.

At this stage it is appropriate to present an example of a simple budget (showing the expected performance of a small house-opening venture once it is set up and running); a break-even budget of the same enterprise; a short cash-flow prediction; and the preparation of some management indices. No attempt has been made to cover the development period, those years through which the business must pass before it is fully established. The 'normal' budget does not, as can be seen, predict immediate and acceptable success. If, nevertheless, the project is to be investigated further, the apparent commercial inadequacies will have to be addressed; the manager should be expected to explain any pitfalls and to indicate where and how performance could be improved over that predicted.

We here enter the mythical world of Nota Manor, a medium sized country house of considerable architectural merit standing in a few acres of garden. It is approached from the main road along a drive which winds through the remains of a wooded parkland now forming part of a farm run by the owner of the house, no doubt through the agency of a farm manager. The house, gardens and farm are themselves part of an agricultural estate, the size and composition of which are, for the purposes of this example, immaterial. The owner of Nota Manor is considering opening the house and gardens to the public with the objective of raising a surplus from the venture sufficiently large to make a sizeable contribution to the costs of repair and upkeep of the house (which at present have to be met out of estate and other income).

The establishment of the venture will entail capital investment on the provision of lavatories for the public; the refurbishment of some accommodation in the house to provide a souvenir shop, tearoom and kitchen; and minor works including the provision in the garden of a children's adventure playground. For the purposes of this example the cost of these various provisions and works is put at £35 000, of which £20 000 will be borrowed at 15% annual interest payable on the amount outstanding at the start of each year.

A budget is required covering one year's operation (on the basis that the business has been established) in order to indicate the extent to which the whole concept is likely to be viable, allowing for the regular paying off of the amount borrowed out of taxed profits. The basis upon which this budget has been prepared is the information contained in the booklet *Going Public* published by the College of Estate Management at Reading which summarizes the results of some ten years research into house-opening ventures undertaken by the authors.

In the preparation of this budget the following assumptions have been made.

1. Visitors admitted in the year: 25 000.
2. Charge for admission per adult: £3 (with unspecified concessions for children, parties and senior citizens), exclusive of VAT (see 7).
3. Income earned by the shop and the tearooms has been put at a figure per visitor admitted to the whole complex and does not represent the amount actually spent by the visitor who buys in the shop or has tea.
4. Staffing to be as follows.

   House

       5 persons covering ticket sales and guides

       2 extra part-time cleaners

       1 extra gardener

       1 part-time car park attendant and general helper

Shop
  2 serving

Tearooms
  3 serving and preparation of teas

5. Management Costs
   On the basis that management is undertaken through the existing estate office

Extra part-time secretarial assistance	£ 4 000
Contribution towards management	£11 800
Legal and audit fees	£ 3 000
Total	£18 800

6. The house and garden will be open to the public for 21 weeks in the year, 5 days a week between 2 pm and 6 pm from May to September.
7. No attempt has been made to provide for the incidence of VAT, partly because the rate of the charge is liable to change over the years but mainly because VAT due on outputs will be set off against VAT re-claimable on an unspecified amount of input tax payable by the estate of which this venture forms a part. In the example, therefore, all trading receipts are shown net of VAT.
8. Tax on net income has been taken at the single figure of 25%.

9.2 EXAMPLE BUDGETS

Normal budget. Admissions 25 000 visitors per annum

Main venture (house)

	£	£
Income		
Ticket sales		
25 000 @ £3 × 83.7%		62 775
Brochure sales @ 1 per 5.5 visitors		
4545 @ £1.50	6 818	
Cost of sales @ 70p	3 181	3 637
Gross profit		66 412
Expenditure		
Less costs		
Guides, ticket sellers, cleaners	10 125	
Car parks, extra gardener	9 060	
Insurance, light, heat, reps furniture, rates	13 200	32 385
PROFIT ON HOUSE		**34 027**

Shop

Income	£	£
Sales, 25 000 @ 60p		15 000
Cost of sales	8 250	8 250
Gross Profit		6 750
Expenditure		
Less other costs		
Staff wages	2 940	
Light, heat, sundries	1 990	4 930
PROFIT ON SHOP		**1 820**

Catering

Income		
Sales @ 75p		18 750
Cost of sales	9 112	9 112
Gross Profit		9 638
Expenditure		
Less other costs		
Staff wages	5 880	
Light, heat, sundries	2 600	8 480
PROFIT ON CATERING		**1 158**

Management

Salaries and fees	18 800
Office and sundries	1 750
Gross Profit	20 550
Advertisements and PR	2 500
Total Management	23 050

Summary

Profit on house	34 027
Profit on shop	1 820
Profit on catering	1 158
	37 005
Less management and advertising	23 050

	£	£
Profit before repairs and interest	**13 995**	
Less Contribution towards repairs	6 000	
	7 955	
Less interest payable	3 000	
Profit before tax	4 955	
Less Income tax @ 25%	1 239	
Profit after tax available to repay loan	**3 716**	

Repayment table (or yearly cash flow)

Year	Loan at start of Year	Profit before interest and tax	Interest	Profit after interest	Tax	Net for repayment	Net as surplus
A. Using surplus as shown above (after contribution towards repairs)							
1	20 000	7 955	3 000	4 955	1 239	3 716	nil
2	16 284	7 955	2 443	5 512	1 378	4 134	nil
3	12 150	7 955	1 823	6 132	1 533	4 599	nil
4	7 551	7 955	1 133	6 822	1 706	5 116	nil
5	2 434	7 955	365	7 590	1 898	2 434	3 258
B. Using surplus only to repay capital (no contribution towards repairs)							
1	20 000	13 955	3 000	10 955	2 739	8 216	nil
2	11 784	13 955	1 768	12 187	3 047	9 140	nil
3	2 644	13 955	397	13 558	3 390	2 644	7 524

Break-even budget

The minimum number of visitors in the year which should produce approximately no profit/no loss is, in round figures 22 000 and a budget based on these figures works out as follows.

Main venture (house)

Income	£	£
Ticket sales		
22 000 @ £3 x 83.7%		55 242
Brochure sales @ 1 per 5.5 visitors		
4545 @ £1.50	6 000	
Cost of sales @ 70p	2 800	3 200
Gross profit		58 442
Expenditure		
All costs as before		32 385
PROFIT ON HOUSE		**26 057**

Shop

Income	£	£
Sales, 22,000 @ 60p		13 200
Costs of sales	7 260	7 260
Gross profit		5 940
Expenditure		
All costs as before (with sundries 10% of costs)		4 831
PROFIT ON SHOP		**1 109**

Catering

Income		
Sales 22,000 @ 76p		16 500
Cost of sales	7 425	7 425
Gross profit		9 075
Expenditure		
All costs as before (with sundries @ 10% of costs)		8 311
PROFIT ON CATERING		**764**

Summary

Profit on house	26 057	
Profit on shop	1 109	
Profit on catering	764	
	27 930	27 930
Less		
Management and advertising as before		23 050
Surplus before repairs and interest		**4 880**
Interest on loan		3 000
Surplus before repairs, income tax or loan repayment		**1 880**

9.3 MANAGEMENT INDICES

A budget once accepted and acted upon must not thereafter gather dust on a shelf. The essence of good management lies in control and that can only be exercised effectively as a result of understanding. It is essential, therefore, for managers to know how the business has performed over the immediate past; certainly year by year (but this is in fact too long a period), preferably month by month or even, if the business is big enough, week by week. The maintenance of weekly records is discussed later on in this chapter. The accepted budget should, therefore, be used for the extraction of management ratios or standards of performance against which management can judge whether performance is as expected or better or worse. As experience builds up, actual performance in previous periods can be compared with current performance. Differences perceived may then alert managers to recent changes in performance, for better or worse, enabling appropriate action to be taken before it is too late.

The customer is, of course, all-important and it is the customer's spending pattern and behaviour which matter as much as, or perhaps more than, how the expenses of the venture are controlled – but both matter. The ratio of income to costs in the various sectors will give a guide to the efficiency of each department of the organization. Exactly which ratios are to be used will depend upon the nature of the enterprise being judged and must be left to senior managers to determine. In the example of the house-opening business shown above, the following indices are suggested as being useful.

House (main venture)

Total costs as percentage of total admissions income

          (32 385 to 62 775)   51.6%

Profit as percentage of turnover

          (34 027 to 69 593)   48.9%

Number of visitors per brochure sold   5.5

Shop

Total costs as percentage of total sales

          (13 180 to 15 000)   87.9%

Profit as percentage of turnover

          (1 820 to 15 000)   12.1%

Rate of turnover of stock $= \dfrac{\text{average stock}}{\text{cost of sales}}$ not available here

Mark-up on goods sold (gross profit on sales)

          (6 750 to 15 000)   45%

Catering

Total costs as percentage of total sales

| | (17 592 to 18 750) | 93.8% |

Profit as percentage of turnover

| | (1 158 to 18 750) | 6.2% |

Rate of stock turnover   not available here

Mark-up on goods sold

| | (9 638 to 18 750) | 51.4% |

Management (with advertising)

Total management costs to gross recreational income

| | (23 050 to 103 343) | 22.3% |

Advertisement costs to total management costs

| | (2 500 to 23 050) | 10.8% |

Advertisement costs to total recreational income

| | (2 500 to 103 343) | 2.4% |

9.4 EXAMPLES OF PERFORMANCE RATIOS

The above indices should remain undisturbed by the impact of inflation and will vary only with changes in management and sales approach. It is interesting however, year by year, to express income and expenditure per visitor in cash terms and their relationship with each other as percentages. For example:

		£
Average expenditure by each visitor	to house	2.78
	in shop	0.60
	in cafe	0.75
Total average expenditure by each visitor		4.13
Profit per visitor per annum from	house	1.36
	shop	0.07
	cafe	0.05
Total profit per visitor before management		1.48
Less management per visitor		0.92
Profit per visitor before interest charges		0.56
Less interest per visitor		0.12
Net profit per visitor		**0.44**

On the basis of these figures it is apparent that 271 visitors are needed to cover each £1000 of costs.

Proportion of expenditure to gross recreational income

	%
(Gross recreational income £103 343)	
House costs (including brochures costs)	34.37
Shop costs	12.75
Catering costs	17.02
Management costs (with advertising)	22.30
Interest	2.90
Profit	**10.66**
	100.00

If the budget is accepted, then an analysis of the budget figures such as that suggested may be used as a measure of performance for the first year or so. If it is not accepted then these figures may give rise to doubt as to the viability of the enterprise and the need for further thought about costs and how to increase profit. In this example for instance, the expenditure on management is a high proportion of the whole; the projected net profit per visitor on the shop and catering is low – will the actual performance work out like this? If so, how may it be increased?

The standards of performance derived from the normal budget are, of course, those which would be thrown up if the venture behaved exactly as predicted in that budget; as such they can only be used to compare the forecast results with those actually achieved. The booklet *Going Public* previously referred to lists performance indices based upon the actual performance of a number of house-opening ventures over a number of seasons. Different recreational ventures may be expected to have different indices which may or may not be readily available to the entrepreneur. Out of interest, a few of the indices given in *Going Public* are reproduced below.

House

Visitors per brochure sold	5.6
Total costs on house as % gross admissions income	63.3%
Cost of paid guides as % gross admissions income	15.2%
Gross admissions income as % adult charge	83.7%

Shop

Net profit to turnover	20.8%
Mark-up on goods sold	41.2%
Times stock turned over in season	1.4

Catering

Net profit to turnover	20.8%
Mark-up on goods sold	53.8%

Management and advertising

Total cost as % gross recreational income	26.5%
Advertising as % gross recreational income	7.8%

Other

Total profit as % total turnover	11.0%

In preparing and using performance figures for the purposes of management control, it is essential to appreciate the reasons for which such control is to be exercised. This throws one back to the management plan for the whole enterprise in which the owner's objectives were set out. The function of management is to achieve those objectives subject to the constraints which will already have been noted – or which have subsequently made themselves apparent. It is easy sometimes for managers from the top downwards, to lose sight of their precise purpose and to manage for the sake of management alone.

It may be, for example, that the objective of management is to make a profit to enable an historic house and garden to be kept up; or to provide local employment; or to enhance the natural beauty of the countryside; or to provide resources for the maintenance and improvement of other land or of agricultural or forestry businesses; or to achieve a number of these objectives. These are mainly linked to the need to build up and run a successful business which is only possible by making available to the public the sort of interest and entertainment for which they are willing to pay. In the public sphere sheer profitability – in whatever worthy cause – may not be an immediate management objective, but efficiency in providing for public enjoyment, will be.

Where profitability is an objective and the enterprise consists of several departments, each charging or selling separately, the manager will need to know more than the overall profit from the whole organization. He or she will need to know, and understand, how each department is faring, what contribution each makes to the whole and which appears to be worth backing or dropping; bearing in mind the extent to which each department is contributing towards the attraction of the whole complex. The provision of teas, for example, may not in itself contribute greatly towards the profits, but if teas were not available many visitors might not come at all. Once the figures of income and expenditure directly attributable to each department are available then considerations other than profitability may hold sway.

Managers however will not be exercising any truly controlling function if their decisions are based solely upon historical records of profit or loss, related, perhaps, to the financial year; by then time for effective action may have passed. The analysis of accounts for management purposes must be over the shortest time possible: this could be weekly for the larger enterprise or monthly for the smaller. The chances are that whether admissions have been high or low the same proportion of people will spend their time and money doing the same things unless and until something alters. Each enterprise, and each department within each enterprise, will therefore find its own pattern and conscious effort will be needed to change it. Where regular records are kept and studied, managers can monitor and evaluate any particular changes in the expected pattern. At the end of each season departmental heads can examine their individual results and prepare budgets for the coming season.

Week by week figures of the gross income and outgoings of each department can be prepared, the turnover calculated and an estimate of gross profit (before overheads) arrived at. These figures relate entirely to the number of people who are attracted to visit the enterprise and to the proportion who visit the particular department concerned. The former number is easily obtained if entry to the complex is by ticket sold at the turnstile, but the number who, for example, come to the shop and buy anything cannot usually be recorded without considerable difficulty; it is necessary therefore to relate most performance figures to the total number of visitors who came through the turnstile for the period concerned.

It may be that such analyses can be used in the first compilation of a cash-flow prediction for a new enterprise, but one must be aware that the experience of one enterprise will not necessarily be reflected in the performance of another and that, as already mentioned, a pilot scheme may be a safer foundation on which to build. In every instance each enterprise discovers that a few people are admitted without being counted or, if counted, without being asked to pay. If this number is small in comparison with the whole they may be ignored. Even so, some analysis of the number is always necessary. Up to what age, for example, are the children admitted free, and how many of them are there? Where some categories of visitors are charged less than the full adult rate or where parties are admitted at concessionary rates some allowance for, or special record of, them may be important.

There will be expenses which the whole enterprise has to meet which do not vary with the number of visitors admitted: for example, insurance premiums, repair costs, maintenance of gardens and the like will remain fairly constant each year whether the enterprise flourishes or fades; indeed some costs will have to be met whether or not the enterprise operates. Other expenses, such as management, cannot be properly allocated to individual departments, and are not directly dependent on admissions (though they will be in the end) but are dependent entirely on the existence of the enterprise. How far these costs are split between departments at the end of the year and how far they are treated as enterprise overheads must be for management to decide. For the purpose of comparison of one enterprise with another, overheads may be broken down to a cost per visitor admitted (which can be a revealing figure).

9.5 RECORD SHEETS

In many cases managers assemble a periodical record sheet which, in simple terms, shows the outcome of the period and how the actual figures compare with the budgeted figures and with the same period in the previous year. In some enterprises a periodical record sheet is prepared for the separate departments to complete weekly or monthly. Departmental outgoings may not be available for these periods (e.g. wages and supplies may be paid for centrally, and supply in particular may be irregular) so that an accurate record of outgoings may only be available at the end of the year. The periodical record sheets tend, of necessity, to concentrate on income rather than on income and expenditure – though of course circumstances alter cases – but can nonetheless provide valuable checks on the progress of the enterprise. A sample record sheet for a week is given below.

Over-sophistication can be self-defeating when too much time is taken up on the production of statistics. Some control can be exercised by the weekly study of figures of turnover. However, such figures will not make immediately comparable the net performance of one sector of the enterprise against the others. A properly compiled record of income and expenditure per visitor admitted over the whole season will enable the declining or increasing popularity of one sector to be seen at once in the changing pattern of visitor outlay and resultant profit. This pattern, as already pointed out, may be distorted if there is a significant number of visitors allowed free admission (and thus perhaps not counted). Reduced admission charges for certain categories of visitor will not affect the pattern significantly (unless the number admitted under such schemes is large); it is however, consideration of this sort of distortion which, if taken to excess, could result in an exasperated abandonment of the collection and refinement of all figures.

Example

Record sheet: for week-ending Sunday (Week No.   )

		This Year	Budget	Last Year
General admissions	No. this week	8 645	9 000	7 976
	No. cumulative from start of season	48 859	47 000	46 213
	Adult/child ratio	1:0.61	1:0.5	1:0.54
House admissions	No. this week	5 385	5 850	4 841
	No. cumulative from start of season	34 934	30 550	27 265
	General/house admission ratio	1:0.71	1:0.65	1:0.59
Shop	Sales this week (£)	1 296	1 260	957
	Cumulative from start of season (£)	5 863	6 110	6 470
	Sales per head this week (p)	45	42	40
	Cumulative from start of season (p)	43	43	41
Catering	Sales this week	£2 766	£2 700	£2 233
	Cumulative from start of season (£)	14 658	14 570	13 863
	Sales per head this week (p)	60	59	55
	Cumulative from start of season (p)	58	58	57
Attractions	Astroglide takings this week (£)	563	525	515
	per head this week (£)	5	4.5	4.7
	Fishing. Value of tickets sold this week (£)	190	210	200

REFERENCES

Centre for Advanced Land Use Studies (1990) *Going Public: An Analysis of House Opening Ventures 1979–1987,* College of Estate Management, Reading.

10.1 BACKGROUND

Interpretation has been defined as 'An educational activity which aims to reveal meaning and relationships through the use of original objects, by first-hand experience and by illustrative media, rather than simply to communicate factual material' (Tilden, 1967). In the spectrum of communication, interpretation lies somewhere between providing basic information and entertainment although the precise boundaries may be blurred. Facilities catering for active recreation such as sports centres or fun parks may need to convey information which might, for example, address safety issues or the use of equipment.

The general approach of interpretation owes much to the educational innovators of the last century who placed great emphasis on experimental learning and the innate desire of participants to learn. Interpretive audiences have no academic prerequisites to satisfy other than 'being there' and, implicitly, having some interest in what is to be learned. This, no doubt, encouraged the growth of guided visits: a method of interpretation developed particularly by the new National Parks Service in the USA during the 1920s. The involvement of a knowledgable guide with visitors represented an important shift away from the dominance of 'showcase' interpretation epitomized by museums and zoos. It is worth dwelling for a moment longer on the role of museums. Created, essentially, to house collections of natural, historic and cultural artifacts, they straddle the area between 'formal' scholarly activity and interpretation. Information presented to the visitor was accurate but purely factual, often requiring considerable prior knowledge on the part of the visitor before full use could be made of the facts. Good interpretation must be based on scholarship. There are many instances, however, where the keeper of a collection is antipathetic towards the visiting public. Such curators consider most visitors to be an unwelcome intrusion into the scholarly activity on which many collections are founded. Nevertheless, most collections are housed and funded by public support and many museums now actively encourage their interpretive role to increase public awareness of the value of their work. This development has been stimulated and assisted by the technological advances achieved in the audio visual presentation of material.

The 'drive' which motivates the recreational visitor is the enjoyment of the visit: interpretation can play an important role in stimulating the response that leads to a fulfilling visit. This in turn helps to reinforce the visitor's perception that the visit is a rewarding experience. Most recreation sites are not perceived instantly and simply, like a supermarket product. A country park may be established in the grounds of a historic mansion whose gardens were designed in the Age of Elegance set in a landscape of great value. On the other hand it might be set in an apparently wild area which arose in the aftermath of mineral extraction of industrial use, creating new but important natural environments. Recreation and interest may be found in the excitement of industrial archaeology, on a footpath in the high hills or on the waters of a new reservoir. In all these cases, and indeed in many more, lies scope for imaginative interpretation providing opportunities for a wide range of benefits to be enjoyed by visitors. Not all visitors will necessarily wish to exploit every benefit to the full. They should, nevertheless, be in a position to make an informed selection of those they do wish to enjoy. Interpretation is intended to promote understanding of the resource through which care and concern may be exercised, but it can also be presented in a way which focuses attention in one direction and away from another. There is much to be gained from enabling visitors to experience a site in a manner which minimizes physical wear and tear on the site without detracting from enjoyment and which indeed often enhances it. Interpretation can play an important role in gaining the understanding and co-operation of visitors in achieving this objective.

National recreation surveys have, for many years, indicated the popularity of informal recreation such as walks in the countryside and visits to historic houses and museums. Almost by definition, a large proportion of the people who embark upon such visits have a poorly defined understanding of:

- the objective of their visit;
- the reasons for the availability of the site;
- how to get the best out of their visit.

Even those who are familiar with the countryside or sites of historic interest often like to increase their knowledge and understanding of them. Consequently, almost any degree of interpretation is likely to be appreciated. However, the art of interpretation is not that of merely delivering information, but of collecting, processing and presenting fact and conjecture imaginatively, so that the visitor becomes interested in and involved with the site, building, artefact or custom being depicted and thus better able to appreciate its significance. Interpretation is not solely confined to the display in a visitor centre: it may be simply a notice *in situ* describing a function or process, scene or event which the visitor sees. Although there is no need for the scene itself to be reproduced or explained, sometimes explanation is difficult, if not impossible. The weaving process, or the progress of a cow through a milking parlour, is more easily understood if it happens before the visitor's eyes than if machinery is static or the essential movement frozen into cold print. Besides, a notice cannot be plied with questions and this is where the guide-interpreter may be an infinitely more effective medium of communication than the notice. Such a person must, however, be fully conversant with the subject matter being interpreted: an ill-informed guide can be worse than no guide at all.

Interpretation requires not only a subject to interpret but a medium for communicating the subject to the intended audience. Although the influence of interpretation on the attraction of some of the most popular recreational destinations such as Colonial Williamsburg, the Epcot centre at Walt Disney World, or Madame Tussauds' Royalty and Empire Museum at Windsor, is self-evident, some managers think of interpretive facilities as non-revenue earning cost centres. This is a misconceived notion; if in doubt, it might be helpful to consider the opportunity cost of interpretation by imagining a site devoid of interpretation and assessing the effect this would have on its ability to attract and interest visitors. Interpretation also plays an important role in making property provided at public expense fully accessible to the general public, encouraging public accountability but, more important, engendering a sense of 'ownership' on the part of the public.

The primary purposes of interpretation may be summarized as follows:

● to provide an enjoyable and rewarding educational experience for visitors;
● to enhance visitors' appreciation and understanding of the site;
● to maximize the carrying capacity of the site and minimize the impact of visitors;
● to promote an understanding of the agency providing or operating the site.

10.2 INTEGRATING INTERPRETATION AND RECREATION

Over the last few years, several examples of sites owing their popularity almost exclusively to interpretation, such as the Jorvik Viking Centre in York or the Ironbridge Gorge Museum in Shropshire, have succeeded consistently in attracting visitor attendances which can be measured in the hundreds of thousands per year. Clearly, enterprises of this size are capable of generating substantial visitor income from admissions. They should be equally capable of generating substantial income from ancillary facilities such as catering and retail sales. The operators of the Jorvik Viking Centre, Cultural Resource Management, encouraged by the financial success of Jorvik, established a parallel business, Heritage Projects, to develop similar interpretive projects in Oxford and Canterbury. The 'profits' from Jorvik are ploughed back into archaeological projects, making the centre one of the major sponsors of British archaeology.

Interpretation will not always be perceived as being a central attraction and may, as often as not, be considered to be an ancillary feature. However, many sites devoted to informal recreation would appear dull and lifeless without interpretation and in these cases it should not be treated as something apart from the main enterprises. It is not difficult to bring to mind examples of day visitor destinations where large numbers of visitors are attracted to a site or artefact of international renown, yet largely denied interpretation; they spend twenty minutes on site, paying a correspondingly meagre admission price, then spend three times as long in the gift shop in the village, laying out proportionately more money in the process. The management principles associated with the provision of interpretive facilities remain the same as for other enterprises designed to attract and then manage the visiting public. There should be:

- a clear mission to provide interpretation;
- clear operational objectives sufficiently precise and unambiguous to be capable of conversion into performance criteria;
- a strategy accompanied by a statement of policy for achieving the operational objectives;
- an action plan for implementing the strategy;
- proper mechanisms for monitoring, control and performance appraisal and review.

One of the most oustanding illustrations of an enterprise centred around interpretation, foremost among the many examples in the USA, if not the world, is Colonial Williamsburg – 'America's favourite outdoor history museum'. Colonial Williamsburg attracts approximately one million visitors per year. Many of them stay in hotels within the historic area owned by the foundation. Admissions income accounts for approximately 20% of total income, while the revenue from hotels and restaurants accounts for a little over 50% of income. The Colonial Williamsburg Foundation employs almost 4 000 people, accounting for over 50% of expenditure. The mission statement which accompanies the current seven year plan for Colonial Williamsburg establishes the following imperatives:

- to restore, recreate, preserve and interpret eighteenth century Williamsburg;
- to teach the history of early America;
- to provide visitors with hospitality, service and products of quality and value.

The importance of interpretation within the mission is clear, but the third imperative is relevant to every enterprise purporting to provide a high quality recreational experience. The Williamsburg plan goes on to identify, explicitly, operational objectives and strategic issues, just as the management plan for any enterprise should. The quality and professionalism of management, from initial market research to final accounting stands as an example for any recreational enterprise.

Williamsburg was designated the colonial capital of Virginia in 1699. At that time the colony of Virginia stretched as far west as the Mississippi River and north to the Great Lakes. From 1699 until 1780 Williamsburg was the political, social and cultural centre of the largest, most populous and, possibly, most influential of the American colonies. Much later, long after Williamsburg had lost its pre-eminence, it became the only colonial capital that was, practically, capable of being restored to its pre-Revolutionary appearance. Restoration of the city began in 1926, funded by the benefaction of John D. Rockefeller Jr. All of the major public buildings of the original city plan still exist or have been reconstructed. A 'living history' programme includes the active practice of 36 colonial crafts and trades, ranging from apothecary to wig-making. Throughout the year, interpreters representing eighteenth century characters provide insights into eighteenth century attitudes, problems and opinions.

The majority of the historic sites comprising Colonial Williamsburg are staffed by people engaged in continuous research. Sometimes progress is rapid; more often it is painfully slow. But regardless of the appearance of new materials and the meticulous reworking of the old, Colonial Williamsburg has always been characterized by a large majority of interpreters trying to learn more about the sites they interpret day in and day out. Colonial Williamsburg has few rivals as a history teacher today. The principles which are followed are explained in *Teaching History at Colonial Williamsburg*, first published in 1985 by the Colonial Williamsburg Foundation and from which the following summary is extracted. The antiquity of the restored colonial city, its completeness, the human scale of its buildings, gardens, streets and lanes, its many pleasing sights, sounds and smells, its reminders of great men doing great deeds in the cause of liberty capture visitors' imaginations and command their senses. Skilled interpreters help visitors see, understand and enjoy their encounters with history. Colonial Williamsburg is a compelling history teacher because it is a place where the past is present, immediately and tangibly present, and a place where history is actively and intelligently interpreted. This wealth of detail, objects and information is not, however, sufficient by itself to make the past comprehensible. The interpretive mix needs a cohesive ingredient; the facts need a plot, the history a conceptual framework. Otherwise the impressions and anecdotes, the demonstrations, tours and presentations cannot yield their full meaning to visitors.

10.3 DEVELOPING AND IMPLEMENTING AN INTERPRETIVE PLAN

Having a mission to undertake something invariably implies commitment, not just to an idea or aim but the commitment of the resources necessary to realize that aim. The resource issues which need to be determined include:

- the size of investment in the basic infrastructure of the interpretive facilities of a site – the number of permanent employees; the amount of fixed capital in buildings and equipment;
- size of investment in 'working capital', bearing in mind that the presentations which are used may have a short 'shelf life' (possibly 2–3 seasons);
- is the interpretation consistent with the overall 'image' which the enterprise is intended to portray?;
- how is the effectiveness of the interpretation to be measured and evaluated?;
- how are the results of this evaluation to be incorporated into the overall management of the enterprise?

Any investment which warrants this level of commitment warrants a plan to map out what should be developed, how it should be developed and how to monitor and evaluate the completed development.

The purpose of interpretation is to provide visitors with a better appreciation of the places, objects, people and cultures they have chosen to experience. The speed with which learning occurs is influenced by several factors such as: the motivation of the visitor; the amount of material to be learned; the time available; the familiarity of the material to the recipient. Other factors which also affect the completeness and speed of the learning process include the media through which the communication processes take place and, of course the design, style and content of the presentation. Good interpretation should stimulate questions from visitors, indeed, these questions can provide an indication of the effectiveness of presentations and displays. They often arise at the end of a visit and thought needs to be given to how they might best be answered and logged, for they provide an important source of information for monitoring the adequacy or inadequacy of the interpretation being provided.

As with so many planning problems the most difficult decision is where to start. The usual dilemma is whether to start by examining the potential of the site for an interpretive programme or to start with the potential audience. The answer is seldom clear-cut and is usually a matter of relative emphasis. In some cases, such as Jorvik, Ironbridge or Colonial Williamsburg, the source material for the site is so rich that the issue becomes a matter of selection and presentation. In most cases such embarrassment of riches does not arise and the general rule must be to give first consideration to the needs of the audience. Thereafter, the sequence of events is outlined

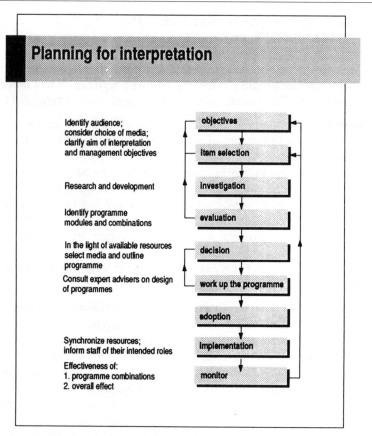

Fig. 10.1 Planning for interpretation.

in a flow chart (Figure 10.1). This illustrates a 'normal' sequence of issues to be considered and the corresponding stages of evaluation and review. However, diagrams such as this fail to emphasize the need to maintain flexibility and choice within a plan. The strength of planning is that it encourages a systematic approach to a complex issue where subjectivity invariably generates problems for future management. Its weakness is that it can produce rules and recommendations cast in tablets of stone which inhibit the evolution of a plan in response to change to which interpretive programmes should be capable of adapting.

In the context of recreational land management, interpretation is normally location-specific, delivered on site about the site, depicting the influences on and characteristics of a site which bestow it with interest and value. In some circumstances the message may place little reliance on a specific location. Indeed, the natural surroundings of a countryside site may encourage the receptivity of audiences toward a broad range of environmental or cultural issues. It can be tempting to tell the visitor too much and perhaps show things which are of supreme interest to the person staging the display but not related to the site. Where plans for an exhibit in a visitor centre veer towards, or indeed take on the form of, a countryside museum or other absorbing display unrelated to the site, the manager should be prepared to confirm the purpose of the display before approving it. This is not to say that unrelated exhibitions should always be prohibited, they might have great drawing-power, but equally they might well have been mounted elsewhere, leaving room for the practice of interpretation to be carried on where it has direct relevance, namely, where the subject lies.

Interpretation must be based on a sound understanding of the subject being interpreted and the audience at which it is directed. Research into the material forming the substance of the interpretation is readily accepted; what is often overlooked is that if the message is misunderstood or not absorbed by the intended audience, it simply represents a waste of effort and investment. Effective interpretation requires effective communication. The message must be appropriate to the subject, the audience and the conditions under which it is to be delivered. It is often assumed by site managers that to make interpretation available is enough: this is misguided. Assuming that the objectives of the interpretive programme for visitor enjoyment, site management and the needs of the operator have been clearly established, the effectiveness of the programme in achieving those objectives must be monitored. It is important to emphasize that the criteria which determine the quality of interpretation may differ, depending on the perspective being adopted, namely, the interpreter, the visitor or the site operator.

Interpretation at Colonial Williamsburg is inspired and shaped by a theme. This helps educational planners write coherent storylines, set priorities, select sites and programmes that make most effective use of the Foundation's resources to achieve its mission. A theme helps interpreters choose what to say and what to leave out. It reminds them that they have a double duty to visitors both to describe life in the past and to explain – according to the chosen theme – how it came to be that way. A common theme also gives direction to research. It sets the agenda of questions to be asked and helps historians select appropriate methods to be employed in answering them. Choosing sites to excavate, collections to acquire and exhibit, and field and documentary studies to conduct can become an exciting collaboration when researchers are guided by the same scholarly compass. The visitor gains too from the incorporation of a theme into interpretation at Colonial Williamsburg. The past is not only presented and described in all its elaborate detail, but its significance and its meaning is also made plain. The past becomes intelligible and, thereby, useful to the visitor. A coherent theme also gives the Foundation's fund-raisers a packaged programme to present to potential donors.

The theme Colonial Williamsburg has chosen to guide its educational programmes over the next decade is called 'Becoming Americans'. The phrase is a shorthand term for a history that a scholarly publication would entitle 'The Evolution of American Society, 1607–1781'. Before interpreters at Colonial Williamsburg can present a new theme to the visiting public, each exhibition site will have to be evaluated for the part that it can most appropriately contribute to the entire story. Separate interpretive plans must be prepared for each exhibition building and craft shop to explain what part of this history of society visitors will encounter at each interpretive station. Descriptive material on each site includes historical information (topics) to be covered in the interpretive presentation and thematic ideas (storylines) to tie the interpretation together. To assist in this selection, The Educational Planning Committee has chosen four topics that provide an appropriate historical context for all exhibition sites and educational programmes. Each subject area (government; work and enterprise; family and community life; cultural life) deals with an aspect of the 'Becoming Americans' theme.

Colonial Williamsburg has a simple geographic focus which means that, in accordance with the management plan, the performance of the enterprise can be kept continually under review. At the other extreme, the USA National Parks Service is responsible for the management of almost four hundred sites, designated by Congress, ranging from the world famous Yellowstone National Park to the ornamental traffic circles in the centre of Washington, DC. The primary objective of the National Parks Service is to manage all properties within the National Park System so that they are left unimpaired for future generations. The demand for new interpretive plans to be prepared for sites of national significance falling within the ambit of the National Park Service is constant. These plans are based on a standardized framework centrally co-ordinated through the National Parks Service Interpretive Design Centre at Harper's Ferry.

The planning process starts, formally, with the production of a development feasibility appraisal and management plan. This results in an interpretive prospectus, essentially a media prescription. The prospectus provides planners of exhibits, audiovisual programmes, wayside information, and historic furnishings with interpretive goals for the site and outlines the route and media vehicles to be used in arriving at those goals. Typically, the Interpretive Prospectus includes the following topics:

- the resource;
- the planning context;
- the market profile and visitor use;
- existing facilities and services;
- interpretive themes and objectives;
- the plan.

Individual components of the interpretive portfolio are designed and produced when funding for a project becomes available. A prospectus seldom contains sufficient detail to guide the individual programme other than specifying appropriate media, such as guided walks, talks, and special events, as being best suited to conveying certain themes. These recommendations are developed at the park level in an interpretive options plan called the 'Statement for Interpretation'.

The interpretive media developed by the National Parks Service have a reputation for being rather conservative and unimaginative. This is partly the result of a resourcing policy which places greater emphasis on satisfying new demands rather than achieving excellence at each and every site. A standardized house style enables production costs to be minimized; it also enables visitors to recognize facilities provided by the National Parks Service from Alaska to Florida. The second reason for an apparently conservative approach to interpretation is that once an interpretive plan has been implemented, it is required to have a long 'shelf life'. Interpretive schemes may have to last twenty years before they are properly reviewed. During this time they must be maintained at the lowest possible cost.

10.4 PERFORMANCE APPRAISAL AND REVIEW

The application of appraisal and review procedures to interpretation requires an appreciation of the extent to which visitor expectations are matched by the interpretation made available to them. The appraisal of interpretation from the perspective of the supplier, particularly which involves or relies on human contact in the form of guides or interpreters, requires a level of self-analysis and self-awareness which does not come naturally to most people. It should, therefore, be handled in a professional and sympathetic manner which encourages staff to analyse their performance within a constructive and supportive environment.

Interpretation which might be considered outstanding from the point of view of the interpreter should:

- be well organized;
- be accurate and relevant, explaining not just 'what' but 'so what';
- be varied in content, method, style, length;
- match personal interests;
- stimulate questions and further study.

Interpretation which might be considered outstanding from the point of view of the visitor will:

- cover the subject, bringing it alive yet placing it in context by relating it to a body of knowledge;

- be informative; accurate; believable; cogent; entertaining; thought provoking;
- provide a new window on the world, encouraging the visitor to lose sense of time.

An interpreter should be:

- knowledgeable (knowing not simply 'the answers' but a lot more) and able to make connections;
- willing and able to contribute to content yet willing to admit that 'we' just don't know everything;
- able to make connections to other sites;
- able to tailor interpretation to visitor needs and be comfortable with the visitors;
- responsive to and learning from visitors;
- friendly, hospitable and courteous; and
- should possess good presentation skills, seeming enthusiastic.

The interpreter needs:

- good feedback from the audience;
- a positive work atmosphere which includes peer support;
- resources to do a good job;
- time free from distraction to undertake the required research.

Presentations should be clear, understandable and convincing. It may seem obvious to say that they should be the 'right' length and have the 'right' content, but these are critical factors – the content of the message should be clear and the timing should be shorter rather than longer. Sometimes it is possible to make an interpretive programme progressive in detail and complexity, giving the audience the ability to proceed further with the content if they require. New technology, particularly in interactive audio-visual systems, make this ideal increasingly attainable, but hitherto, the only way of tailoring detail and complexity to visitor requirements has been to use live interpretation. It should appear new and fresh-sounding. It should include and involve each visitor, encouraging questions and giving answers. The audience should be comfortable – physically and mentally (i.e. reinforces existing attitudes and ideas). At the end of the presentation visitors should feel that it was special and professional.

10.5 CONCLUSION

The role and effectiveness of interpretation must always be judged in relation to the original objectives set for the enterprise. There is a danger of providing interpretation for the sake of it, resulting in, possibly, superb interpretation but inconsistent with the aims of the site. This raises the dangerous possibility of interpretation being used to justify site management which has lost or never had a clear direction. This point is graphically illustrated by a conversation between an environmental scientist and the author Alston Chase, (Chase, 1987).

'Interpreters exist only to apologise for Park Service mistakes. Consider a recent incident that occurred in Hawaii: the Superintendent of City of Refuge National Park on the island of Hawaii was walking on the beach of the Park with his Chief Naturalist and a visiting Park Service scientist. The ground there was sacred to the natives, to whom it had been a sanctuary, much as churches were in the West. Its beach had been kept as one of the most pristine in the world. As the three men walked the shore they came to a two hole outhouse. Beneath the outhouse and descending across the sand to the ocean was a yellow stream of urine. In the ocean where the two bodies of water met was a gigantic algae bloom.

'What the hell is going on here?' asked the scientist.

The Superintendent, embarrassed, looked at his Chief Naturalist.

'That's all right,' said the naturalist, 'we'll interpret it for the public.'

'Interpret, hell,' replied the scientist. 'Get it the f*** off the beach!'

REFERENCES

Chase, A. (1987) *Playing God in Yellowstone*, Harcourt Brace and Jovanovich, San Diego, New York, London.

Tilden, F. (1967) *Interpreting Our Heritage*, University of North Carolina Press, California.

Index